SOUPS
BEST-EVER SOUPS RECIPES

SOUPS
BEST-EVER SOUPS RECIPES

bay books

RECIPE PLANNER

Use the following table to select your best ever Soup recipe. The recipes have been grouped into appropriate classifications and the portion size of each recipe is clearly shown. Choose your soup and then turn to the appropriate page to find your clear and concise recipe together with a large-format picture of the finished dish.

BEEF, LAMB & PORK

RECIPE	PAGE	PORTIONS
Beef consomme	113	4-6
Beef pho	114	4
Chickpea, chorizo and pork rib soup	125	6-8
Grilled Italian sausage and vegetable soup	133	4
Hot and sour lime soup with beef	134	4
Lamb and pasta soup	141	6-8
Long and short noodle soup	145	6
Moroccan lamb, chickpea and coriander soup	146	4-6

CHICKEN & POULTRY

RECIPE	PAGE	PORTIONS
Curried chicken noodle soup	35	4
Avgolemono with chicken	110	4
Chicken and couscous soup	117	6
Chicken and galangal soup	118	4
Chicken and vegetable soup	121	6-8
Chicken, mushroom and Madeira soup	122	4
Creamy chicken and corn soup	126	4-6
Duck, shiitake mushrooms and rice noodle broth	129	4-6
Five-spice duck and somen noodle soup	130	4
Thai-style chicken and coconut soup	137	4
Jungle soup	138	4
Lemon chicken soup	142	4
Mulligatawny soup	149	4-6
Spicy chicken broth with coriander pasta	165	4

Oxtail soup with stout and vegetables	150	4
Pea and ham soup	153	6-8
Pork and buttered corn ramen soup	154	4
Pork congee	157	4-6
Rustic hot pot	158	4
Scotch broth	161	8
Spaghetti and meatball soup	162	4
Spicy lamb soup	166	4-6
Vietnamese beef soup	170	4
Beef and beet borscht	189	4

Tom kha gai	169	4
Miso soup with chicken and udon noodles	182	4

FISH & SEAFOOD

RECIPE	PAGE	PORTIONS
Bouillabaisse	12	4-6
Clam chowder	15	4
Lobster bisque	16	4
Mediterranean fish soup	19	6-8
Prawn gumbo	20	4
Saffron fish soup	23	4
Seafood ravioli in gingery soup	24	4

There's nothing quite like homemade soup. It's enjoyable and surprisingly easy to make if you follow a few commonsense rules, and can be dressed up or down to suit just about any occasion.

The French quotation states 'soup is to dinner what the gateway is to a building', meaning that the soup should be chosen carefully to lead the diners into the meal. With some soups, such as consommés and light broths, this is still the case, but many others have become delicious, nutritious, flavour-packed meals in their own right. Today there are many different types of soup, varying in preparation, creaminess and consistency. We have broths, chowders, bouillons, consommés, as well as all manner of creamy soups.

The story goes that the most famous soup of all, Minestrone, was first tasted during the Crusades when Italian soldiers boiled up meat in water to make a simple broth, then asked the neighbouring villagers to contribute vegetables and herbs. Such humble beginnings for one of the world's most popular dishes.

STOCK SECRETS

While soup is the ideal vehicle for using up odds and ends from the refrigerator, it is only as good as its ingredients, and the backbone of any good soup is its stock. There are several alternatives when choosing stock. You can use home-made, fresh or frozen stock available from some delicatessens or poultry shops, or tetra packs or cubes from the supermarket. The best stock will be home-made or fresh and, as it can be frozen, it is a good idea to cook up large quantities every time. Tetra packs are convenient, as are stock cubes; however, check the labels and choose cubes made from natural ingredients with no added MSG. Commercial stocks always tend to be much saltier than home-made, so taste the soup before seasoning with salt and pepper. Always season soup at the end of the cooking time, as long cooking concentrates the flavours.

Try to use the flavour stock called for in the recipe. A beef stock would be overpowering in a recipe that calls for chicken stock, although vegetarians might prefer to use vegetable stock in all their soups.

PUREEING AND STRAINING

Many soups are puréed before serving and there is a sensible way to go about this. Let the soup cool a little first, so that it is safe if it

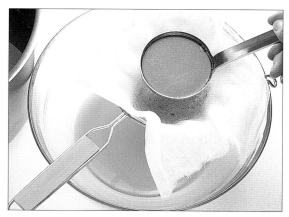

Clear soups can be strained through a sieve lined with damp muslin.

Some soups thicken on standing and need to be diluted when they are reheated.

splashes. Cool it quickly by pouring it into a bowl, then wash the pan to take the puréed soup for reheating. Purée in either a food processor or a blender – a blender will give a finer result, though it tends to aerate the soup slightly. Always purée in batches, never filling the processor above halfway.

Occasionally, recipes ask for the soup to be strained, particularly if making the stock is part of the recipe. A fine sieve (not a colander) is usually adequate. Some clear soups need more than one straining, through a sieve lined with damp muslin. If you don't have muslin, use a clean damp chux (kitchen cloth).

AHEAD OF TIME

Many soups can be made in advance and do, in fact, benefit from overnight refrigeration as the flavours develop. Use commonsense to determine if any of the ingredients will not store well, for example if the soup has cream, add it when you are reheating for serving. The same goes for pasta; for instance, if you add the pasta to Minestrone, then leave it to sit around, it will be unpleasantly soggy. Generally, soups can be kept for up to 3 days in the refrigerator, or frozen in airtight containers or freezer bags for up to 1–3 months. A lot of soups become very thick on standing and need to be diluted when reheated. Use more of the same stock, water or cream, as appropriate. The seasoning will also need to be adjusted.

SIMMERING SOUPS

Most recipes call for a heavy-based pan for making soup. This is so that the pan distributes heat evenly and prevents anything 'catching' on the bottom. A wide, shallow pan will allow too much evaporation. The recipe will state if the pan should be covered. If it is not to be covered the soup will simmer and, as the liquid evaporates off it, it will reduce down and thicken. So, if your soup is still a little thin, simply simmer it uncovered for a while. Most soups are cooked at a gentle simmer, meaning that the surface of the soup is barely moving, while a simmer means the soup will be moving faster but without bubbles breaking the surface. Boiling is when bubbles actively break the surface of the soup. Watch the soup and adjust the heat accordingly. If the recipe says to partially cover the pan, tilt the lid at an angle so that there is a gap for steam to escape.

Bubbles will be breaking on the surface when the soup is boiling.

Tilt the lid at an angle if the recipe calls for a partially covered pan.

7

Soup is a dish whose sum is definitely greater than its parts. And one of its most important parts is stock. A good stock makes the difference between an ordinary and a spectacular soup, giving full-bodied flavours and a sound base for the other ingredients. If you are looking at these recipes and thinking the cooking times seeming very long and it all looks like too much trouble, think again. It doesn't take long to chop up the ingredients and then you can leave your stock to simmer lazily while you get on with other things.

BEEF STOCK

2 kg (4 lb) beef bones; 2 unpeeled carrots, chopped; 2 unpeeled onions, quartered; 2 tablespoons tomato paste; 2 sticks celery, leaves included, chopped; 1 bouquet garni, 12 black peppercorns

1 Preheat the oven to hot 210°C (415°F/Gas 6–7). Put the bones in a baking dish and bake for 30 minutes, turning occasionally. Add the carrot and onion and cook for a further 20 minutes. Allow to cool.

2 Put the bones, carrot and onion in a large, heavy-based pan. Drain the excess fat from the baking dish and pour 1 cup (250 ml/8 fl oz) of water into the dish. Stir to dissolve any juices; add the liquid to the pan.

3 Add the tomato paste, celery and 10 cups (2.5 litres/85 fl oz) water. Bring to the boil, skimming the surface as required and add the bouquet garni and peppercorns. Reduce the heat to low and simmer gently for four hours. Skim the froth from the surface regularly.

4 Ladle the stock in batches into a fine sieve sitting over a bowl. Gently press the solids with a ladle to extract all the liquid. Discard the bones and vegetables and set aside to cool. Refrigerate until cold and spoon off any fat that has set on top. At this stage you can reduce the stock to concentrate its flavour (dilute before using) and store in the refrigerator for up to 2 days or in the freezer for up to 6 months.

Beef stock, chicken stock, fish stock, vegetable stock

2 kg (4 lb) chicken bones; 2 unpeeled onions, quartered; 2 unpeeled carrots, chopped; 2 sticks celery, leaves included, chopped; 1 bouquet garni; 12 black peppercorns

1 Put the chicken bones, onion, carrot, celery and 14 cups (3.5 litres/118 fl oz) of water in a large, heavy-based pan. Bring slowly to the boil. Skim the surface as required and add the bouquet garni and peppercorns. Reduce the heat to low and simmer gently for 3 hours. Skim the froth from the surface regularly.

2 Ladle the stock in batches into a fine sieve sitting over a bowl. Gently press the solids with a ladle to extract all the liquid. Let the stock cool, then refrigerate until cold and spoon off any fat that has set on the top. At this stage you can reduce the stock to concentrate its flavour (dilute before using) and store in the refrigerator for up to 2 days or in the freezer for up to 6 months.

2 kg (4 lb) chopped fish bones, heads and tails; 1 stick celery, leaves included, roughly chopped; 1 onion, chopped; 1 unpeeled carrot, chopped; 1 leek, sliced; 1 bouquet garni; 12 black peppercorns

1 Place the fish bones, celery, onion, carrot, leek and 8 cups (2 litres/68 fl oz) water in a large, heavy-based pan. Bring slowly to the boil. Skim the surface as required and add the bouquet garni and peppercorns. Reduce the heat to low and simmer very gently for 20 minutes. Skim the froth from the surface regularly.

2 Ladle the stock in batches into a sieve line with damp muslin sitting over a bowl. To keep a clear fish stock, do not press the solids, but simply allow the stock to strain undisturbed.

Allow to cool, then store in the refrigerator for up to 2 days or in the freezer for up to 6 months.

1 tablespoon oil; 1 onion, chopped; 2 leeks, chopped; 4 carrots, chopped; 2 parsnips, chopped; 4 sticks celery, leaves included, chopped; 2 bay leaves; 1 bouquet garni; 4 unpeeled cloves garlic; 8 black peppercorns

1 Heat the oil in a large, heavy-based pan and add the onion, leek, carrot, parsnip and celery. Cover and cook for 5 minutes without colouring. Add 12 cups (3 litres/118 fl oz) of water. Bring to the boil. Skim the surface if required, and add the bay leaves, bouquet garni, garlic and peppercorns. Reduce the heat to low and simmer for 1 hour. Skim the froth from the surface of the stock regularly.

2 Ladle the stock in batches into a fine sieve sitting over a bowl. Gently press the solids to extract all the liquid.

3 Allow the stock to cool, then refrigerate until cold and spoon off any fat that has set on the top. At this stage you can reduce the stock to concentrate its flavour (dilute before using) and store in the refrigerate for up to 2 days or in the freezer for up to 6 months.

If you are preparing soup to serve as a dinner party starter or as a main course meal for the family, liven it up a little by adding bowls of accompaniments in the centre of the table. People can pick and choose what to add to their own bowl of soup. Croutons and Garlic Sippets are a delicious way to add extra texture and interest to just about any soup. Rouille and Aioli are best known as creamy, garlicky toppings for fish soups. Harissa is great for spicing up pumpkin soup and Pesto is perfect on thick vegetable soups. You could try serving toppings with stews as well.

AIOLI

Put 2 egg yolks in a food processor. Add 3 peeled, crushed cloves of garlic and 2 teaspoons lemon juice and process for 20 seconds. With the motor running add 250 ml (1 cup/8 fl oz) light olive oil in a thin steady stream and continue processing until the mixture is thick and creamy. Add 2 extra teaspoons of lemon juice and season to taste. Aioli is served in dollops on top of soups and can be stored in an airtight container in the refrigerator for up to 3 weeks.

GARLIC SIPPETS

Trim the crusts from 3 slices of white or brown bread and cut the bread into small cubes. Heat 60 ml ($^1/_4$ cup/2 fl oz) olive oil in a small, heavy-based pan. Add 1–2 crushed cloves of garlic. When the oil is moderately hot add the bread cubes in batches. Cook until golden and crisp, then remove from the pan with a slotted spoon and leave to drain on paper towels while frying the rest. Sprinkle over soup.

PESTO

Put 2–3 cloves of garlic, 60 g (2 cups/2 oz) of fresh basil leaves, 50 g ($^1/_2$ cup) of freshly grated Parmesan cheese, 2 tablespoons toasted pinenuts and 125 ml ($^1/_2$ cup/4 fl oz) of olive oil in a food processor. Process to form a paste, adding a little extra oil to thin if

necessary. Spoon the pesto sparingly over soup in serving bowls. Store in an airtight, screw-top jar. Pack the pesto firmly into the jar and pour in enough extra olive oil to cover the surface. Refrigerate for up to 2 weeks.

ROUILLE

Remove the crusts from 4 thick slices of white bread. Put the bread in a bowl and just cover with water. Leave to soak for 5 minutes then drain, squeezing out the water. Put the bread in a food processor with 4 cloves of garlic, 2 chopped red chillies, 2 egg yolks, salt and pepper. Process for 20 seconds and then, with the motor still running, add 185 ml ($^3/_4$ cup/ 6 fl oz) of olive oil in a thin steady stream. Process until thick and creamy, adding 1 small peeled red capsicum (pepper) if you like. Serve in dollops on top of fish soups.

Hint: To peel a capsicum, cut in half and remove the seeds and membrane. Brush the skin with a little oil and grill (broil), skin side up, under high heat until the skin blackens. Leave to cool under a clean tea towel, then peel away the skin and discard.

HARISSA

Split 100 g ($3^1/_2$ oz) dried red chillies in half and remove the seeds—wear rubber or cotton gloves to do this or later you'll rub your eyes or mouth and find them smarting with hot chilli.

Place the chillies in hot water to soften and rehydrate slightly. Drain the chillies and put them in a food processor or blender with 6 cloves of garlic, 4 tablespoons salt, 50 g ($^1/_2$ cup/$1^3/_4$ oz) of ground coriander and 35 g ($^1/_3$ cup/$1^1/_4$ oz) of ground cumin. Process for 30 seconds. Add 170 ml ($^2/_3$ cup/$5^3/_4$ fl oz) of olive oil in a thin steady stream, processing as you do so until the mixture forms a paste. Store in an airtight screw-top jar in the refrigerator. Add sufficient Harissa to enhance the flavour of the soup, stirring in a little at a time.

CROUTONS

Discard the crusts from 3–4 slices of white or brown bread. Combine 2–3 tablespoons olive

oil and 1–2 peeled, crushed cloves of garlic in a small bowl, then use to brush both sides of the bread. Cut the bread into small cubes and put them on an oven tray. Bake in a preheated 180°C (350°F/Gas 4) oven for 10–15 minutes, or until golden. Allow to cool before serving on top of soups.

Variations: Omit the garlic or add $^1/_2$–1 teaspoon of any ground spice to the oil for an alternative flavour. Croutons can also be made without using any oil. Simply toast the bread cubes in the oven until golden.

GARNISHES

11

BOUILLABAISSE

4–6 tomatoes
500 g (1 lb) raw king prawns
1 raw lobster tail
1–2 fish heads
1 cup (250 ml/8 fl oz) red wine
3 onions, finely chopped
6 cloves garlic, crushed
3 bay leaves
$1/4$ cup (60 ml/2 fl oz) olive oil
1 leek, finely sliced
$1/4$ cup (60 g/2 oz) tomato paste
small piece of orange rind
500 g (1 lb) white fish fillet, cut into small pieces
12 mussels, firmly closed, scrubbed and beards removed
200 g ($6^1/_2$ oz) scallops with corals
$1/2$ cup (30 g/1 oz) chopped parsley
$1/4$ cup (15 g/$^1/_2$ oz) shredded basil leaves

1 Score a cross in the base of each tomato. Cover with boiling water for 1 minute, plunge in cold water, drain and peel away the skins.

2 To make the fish stock, peel and devein prawns and set shells, heads and tails aside. Shell lobster tail, keeping shell and chopping meat. Put lobster shell, fish heads, prawn shells, heads and tails in a large pan. Add wine, 1 onion, 2 cloves garlic, 1 bay leaf and 2 cups (500 ml/16 fl oz) of water. Bring to the boil, reduce heat and simmer for 20 minutes. Strain through a fine sieve, reserving stock.

3 Heat oil in a large, heavy-based pan. Add leek and remaining onion and garlic. Cover and simmer, stirring occasionally, over low heat for 20 minutes, or until browned. Add the tomato, remaining bay leaves, tomato paste and orange rind and stir well. Remove lid and continue to cook for 10 minutes, stirring occasionally. Add the reserved fish stock, bring to the boil, reduce the heat and simmer for 10 minutes, stirring occasionally.

4 Add prawns, lobster, fish pieces, mussels and scallops. Simmer, covered, for 4–5 minutes. Discard any unopened mussels, the rind and bay leaves. Add the herbs and season to taste with salt and freshly ground black pepper. The Bouillabaisse is shown here with a bowlful of Rouille, a delicious accompaniment.

INGREDIENTS

1.5 kg (3 lb 5 oz) fresh clams (vongole) in shell
1 tablespoon oil
3 rashers bacon, chopped
1 onion, chopped
1 garlic clove, crushed
4 potatoes, cubed
310 ml (1^1/$_4$ cups) fish stock
500 ml (2 cups) milk
125 ml (^{1}/$_2$ cup) cream
15 g (^{1}/$_4$ cup) chopped fresh parsley

1   Discard any clams which are already open. Put the remainder in a large heavy-based pan with 250 ml (1 cup/8 fl oz) water and simmer, covered, over low heat for 5 minutes, or until the shells open (discard any clams which do not open during cooking). Strain the liquid and reserve. Remove the clam meat from the shells, discarding the shells.

2   Heat the oil in a clean pan and then add the bacon, onion and garlic. Cook, stirring, until the onion is soft and the bacon golden. Add the potato and stir to combine.

3   Measure the reserved clam liquid and add enough water to make it up to 310 ml (1^1/$_4$ cups/10^1/$_2$ fl oz). Add this to the pan with the stock and milk. Bring to the boil and then reduce the heat, cover and simmer for 20 minutes, or until the potato is tender.

4   Uncover and leave to simmer for a further 10 minutes, or until reduced and slightly thickened. Add the cream, clam meat, salt and pepper to taste and parsley. Heat through gently before serving but do not allow to boil or the flavour will be impaired.

LOBSTER BISQUE

400 g (13 oz) raw lobster tail
100 g (3^1/$_2$ oz) butter, softened
7 spring onions, chopped
1 onion, chopped
1 carrot, chopped
4 cups (1 litre/34 fl oz) fish stock
4 sprigs parsley
1 bay leaf
4 peppercorns
^{1}/$_3$ cup (40 g/1^1/$_4$ oz) plain (all-purpose) flour
1^3/$_4$ cups (440 ml/14 fl oz) tomato paste (purée)
1 tablespoon sherry, optional
^{1}/$_2$ cup (125 ml/4 fl oz) cream
pinch of nutmeg
2 teaspoons chopped tarragon

1 Cut the lobster tail in half lengthways. Melt half the butter in a pan, add the spring onion and onion and cook for 5 minutes, or until soft but not coloured. Add the carrot and cook for 2 minutes. Add the lobster halves, fish stock, parsley, bay leaf, peppercorns and 2^1/$_2$ cups (600 ml/20 fl oz) of water. Bring to the boil, reduce the heat and simmer for 20 minutes, skimming the surface as required.

2 Remove the lobster from the stock, cool slightly and take the meat from the shells. Crush the shells and return to the pan. Continue simmering for a further 40 minutes. Strain the stock, then strain again through a sieve lined with 2 layers of damp muslin.

3 Cut some thin slices from the lobster to use as a garnish and set aside. In a blender, blend the remaining lobster flesh with a little of the strained stock until smooth. Mix the flour and remaining butter to a paste. Add the puréed lobster to the pan along with the flour paste, tomato purée, sherry, cream, nutmeg and salt and pepper, to taste. Mix well.

4 Add the tarragon and remaining stock and cook, stirring continuously, over high heat until the soup boils and thickens. Reduce the heat and simmer gently for 5 minutes. Season to taste and serve garnished with the reserved lobster and some sprigs of tarragon, if you want.

INGREDIENTS

1 kg (2 lb 4 oz) white fish fillets
60 ml ($^1/_4$ cup) olive oil
2 large onions, chopped
1–2 garlic cloves, crushed
4 large tomatoes, peeled, seeded and chopped
2 tablespoons tomato paste (purée)
6 tablespoons chopped gherkins
1 tablespoon chopped capers
1 tablespoon pitted and chopped green olives
1 tablespoon pitted and chopped black olives
750 ml (3 cups) fish stock
250 ml (1 cup) white wine
1 bay leaf
15 g ($^1/_4$ cup) chopped fresh basil
60 g (1 cup) chopped fresh parsley

1 Remove the skin and bones from the fish and chop into bite-sized pieces. Heat the oil in a large heavy-based pan and cook the onion and garlic for 8 minutes until soft.

2 Stir in the tomato and paste. Stir for 2–3 minutes, or until the tomato is soft. Stir in the gherkins and half the capers and olives.

3 Add the fish, stock, wine and bay leaf and season. Bring slowly to the boil, reduce the heat and simmer for 10–12 minutes, or until the fish is just cooked. Stir in the herbs. Add the remaining capers and olives. Serve.

PRAWN GUMBO

2 tablespoons olive oil

1 large onion, finely chopped

3 garlic cloves, crushed

1 red capsicum (pepper), chopped

4 rashers bacon, chopped

$1^1/_2$ teaspoons dried thyme

2 teaspoons dried oregano

1 teaspoon paprika

$^1/_2$ teaspoon cayenne pepper

60 ml ($^1/_4$ cup) sherry

1 litre (4 cups) fish stock

100 g ($^1/_2$ cup) long-grain rice

2 bay leaves

400 g (14 oz) can chopped tomatoes

150 g ($5^1/_2$ oz) okra, thinly sliced

850 g (1 lb 14 oz) medium raw prawns (shrimp), peeled and deveined

3 tablespoons finely chopped flat-leaf (Italian) parsley

1 Heat the oil in a large saucepan over low heat. Cook the onion, garlic, capsicum and bacon for 5 minutes, or until soft. Stir in the herbs and spices. Season. Add the sherry and cook until evaporated, then add the stock and 500 ml (2 cups) water. Bring to the boil. Add the rice and bay leaves, reduce the heat and simmer, covered, for 20 minutes.

2 Add the tomato and okra. Simmer, covered, for 20–25 minutes. Stir in the prawns and parsley and simmer for 5 minutes, or until the prawns are cooked through.

INGREDIENTS

1 kg (2 lb) white fish bones (heads and trimmings), chopped
2 cups (500 ml/16 fl oz) dry white wine
1 onion, chopped
1 carrot, chopped
1 stick celery, chopped
1 bay leaf
6 black peppercorns
$3/4$ teaspoon saffron threads
50 g ($1^3/4$ oz) butter
$1/4$ cup (30 g/1 oz) plain (all-purpose) flour
12 scallops, trimmed
250 g (8 oz) boneless white fish fillets, cut into cubes
1 cup (250 ml/8 fl oz) cream

1   To make the saffron fish stock, place the fish bones, 3 cups (750 ml/24 fl oz) of water, the wine, onion, carrot, celery, bay leaf and peppercorns in a large pan. Bring to the boil slowly, skimming the surface as required. Simmer, covered, for 20 minutes. Strain and discard the fish and vegetables. Take 4 cups (1 litre) of the hot stock and stir in the saffron threads. (If you have any stock leftover at this stage, you can simply freeze it for use in another recipe.)

2   Melt the butter in a large pan and stir in the flour. Cook, stirring continuously, over low heat for 3 minutes but do not allow the mixture to colour. Remove from the heat and gradually pour in the reserved fish stock. Return to the heat and stir continuously until the mixture boils and thickens slightly. Add the scallops and fish cubes, bring back to the boil and simmer for 1–2 minutes.

3   Stir in the cream and reheat gently, but do not allow the soup to boil. Season to taste with salt and freshly ground white pepper. Garnish with sprigs of chervil, if you want.

SEAFOOD RAVIOLI IN GINGERY SOUP

INGREDIENTS

8 raw prawns (shrimp)
1 carrot, chopped
1 onion, chopped
1 celery stick, chopped
3 spring onions, thinly sliced
6 cm (2$^1/_2$ inch) piece fresh ginger, thinly shredded
1 tablespoon mirin
1 teaspoon kecap manis
1 tablespoon soy sauce
4 large scallops
100 g (3$^1/_2$ oz) boneless white fish fillet
1 egg white
200 g (6$^1/_2$ oz) round gow gee wrappers
$^1/_3$ cup (10 g/$^1/_4$ oz) fresh coriander (cilantro) leaves

1 To make the soup, peel the prawns, reserve 4 for the ravioli filling and chop the rest into small pieces and reserve. Put the prawn heads and shells in a large pan, cook over high heat until starting to brown, then cover with 1 litre water. Add the carrot, onion and celery, bring to the boil, reduce the heat and simmer for 10 minutes. Strain and discard the prawn heads, shells and vegetables. Return the stock to a clean pan and add the spring onion, ginger, mirin, kecap manis and soy sauce. Set aside.

2 To make the ravioli, chop the whole reserved prawns with the scallops and fish in a food processor until smooth. Add enough egg white to bind. Lay half the gow gee wrappers on a work surface and place a rounded teaspoon of filling in the centre of each. Brush the edges with water. Top each with another wrapper and press the edges to seal, eliminating air bubbles as you go. Trim with a fluted cutter. Cover with plastic wrap.

3 Bring a large pan of water to the boil. Meanwhile, heat the stock and leave simmering. Just prior to serving, drop a few ravioli at a time into the boiling water. Cook for 2 minutes, remove with a slotted spoon and divide among heated bowls. Cook the chopped reserved prawns in the same water for 2 minutes; drain. Pour the hot stock over the ravioli and serve, sprinkled with the chopped cooked prawns and coriander leaves.

INGREDIENTS

500 g (1 lb) smoked haddock
1 potato, diced
1 stick celery, diced
1 onion, finely chopped
50 g (1^3/$_4$ oz) butter
1 rasher bacon, rind removed and finely chopped
2 tablespoons plain (all-purpose) flour
^{1}/$_2$ teaspoon dried mustard
^{1}/$_2$ teaspoon Worcestershire sauce
1 cup (250 ml/8 fl oz) milk
^{1}/$_2$ cup (15 g/^{1}/$_2$ oz) chopped parsley
^{1}/$_4$ cup (60 ml/2 fl oz) cream (optional)

1   To make the fish stock, put the fish in a frying pan, cover with water and bring to the boil.
    Reduce the heat and simmer for 8 minutes, or until the fish flakes easily. Drain, reserving
    the fish stock, then peel, bone and flake the fish. Set aside.

2   Put the potato, celery and onion in a medium pan and pour over enough reserved fish
    stock to cover the vegetables. Bring to the boil, reduce the heat and simmer for 8 minutes,
    or until the vegetables are tender. Set aside.

3   Melt the butter in a large pan, add the bacon and cook, stirring, for 3 minutes. Add the
    flour, mustard and Worcestershire sauce and stir until combined. Cook for 1 minute.
    Remove from the heat and gradually pour in the milk, stirring continuously, until smooth.
    Return to the heat and stir for 5 minutes, until the mixture comes to the boil and has
    thickened. Stir in the vegetables and remaining stock, then add the parsley and fish.
    Simmer over low heat for 5 minutes, or until heated through. Taste for seasoning and serve
    with some cream, if you want.

INGREDIENTS

2 corn cobs (700 g/1 lb 9 oz)
1 tablespoon olive oil
1 red onion, finely chopped
1 small red chilli, finely chopped
$1/2$ teaspoon ground allspice
4 vine-ripened tomatoes, peeled and finely diced
1.5 litres (6 cups) fish stock or light chicken stock
300 g ($10^1/_2$ oz) boneless firm white fish fillets (ling or
    perch), diced
200 g (7 oz) fresh crab meat
200 g (7 oz) peeled raw prawns (shrimp), roughly chopped
1 tablespoon lime juice

Quesadillas
4 flour tortillas (19 cm/$7^1/_2$ in)
85 g ($^2/_3$ cup) grated Cheddar cheese
4 tablespoons coriander (cilantro) leaves
2 tablespoons olive oil

1 Preheat the oven to 200°C (400°F/Gas 6). Peel back the husks on the corn cobs (making sure they stay intact at the base) and remove the silks. Fold the husks back over the corn, place in a baking dish and bake for 1 hour, or until the corn is tender.

2 Heat the oil in a large saucepan over medium heat. Add the onion and cook until soft. Add the chilli and allspice and cook for 1 minute, then add the tomato and stock and bring to the boil. Reduce the heat and simmer, covered, for 45 minutes.

3 Slice off the kernels from the corn cobs with a sharp knife, add to the soup and simmer, uncovered, for 15 minutes. Add the fish, crab and prawn meat to the soup and simmer for 5 minutes, or until the seafood is cooked. Stir in the lime juice and serve with the quesadillas, if desired.

4 To make the quesadillas, top one tortilla with half the cheese and half the coriander. Season, then top with another tortilla. Heat 1 tablespoon of the oil in a frying pan and cook the quesadilla for 30 seconds on each side, or until the cheese just begins to melt. Repeat to make the other quesadilla. Cut into wedges.

INGREDIENTS

500 g (1 lb) raw prawns (shrimp)
1 tablespoon oil
2 tablespoons tom yam curry paste
2 tablespoons tamarind purée
2 teaspoons ground turmeric
1 teaspoon chopped small red chillies
4 kaffir lime (makrut) leaves, shredded
2 tablespoons fish sauce
2 tablespoons lime juice
2 teaspoons grated palm sugar or soft brown sugar
kaffir lime (makrut) leaves, shredded, extra, to garnish

1   Peel the prawns, leaving the tails intact. Devein the prawns, starting at the head end. Reserve the shells and heads. Cover and refrigerate the prawn meat. Heat the oil in a wok or large saucepan and cook the shells and heads over medium heat, stirring frequently, for 10 minutes, or until the shells turn orange.

2   Add 1 cup (250 ml/8 fl oz) water and the tom yam paste to the pan. Bring to the boil and cook for 5 minutes, or until reduced slightly. Add another 2 litres water, bring to the boil, reduce the heat and simmer for 20 minutes. Strain, discarding the shells and heads, and return the stock to the pan.

3   Add the tamarind, turmeric, chilli and lime leaves to the pan, bring to the boil and cook for 2 minutes. Add the prawns and cook for 5 minutes, or until pink. Stir in the fish sauce, lime juice and sugar. Garnish with shredded kaffir lime leaves.

ASIAN NOODLE SOUP

INGREDIENTS

8 dried Chinese mushrooms
100 g (3^1/$_2$ oz) dried rice vermicelli
800 g (1 lb 12 oz) Chinese broccoli, cut into 5 cm (2 inch) lengths
8 fried tofu puffs, cut into strips
125 g (4^1/$_2$ oz) bean sprouts
1 litre (4 cups) vegetable stock
2 tablespoons light soy sauce
1^1/$_2$ tablespoons Chinese rice wine
3 spring onions (scallions), finely chopped
coriander (cilantro) leaves, to serve

1   Place the dried mushrooms in a bowl, cover with boiling water and soak for 15 minutes. Drain, reserving 125 ml (^{1}/$_2$ cup) of the liquid. Squeeze the mushrooms to remove any excess liquid. Discard the stems and thinly slice the caps.

2   Soak the vermicelli in boiling water for 5 minutes. Drain. Divide the vermicelli, broccoli, tofu puffs and bean sprouts among the four serving bowls.

3   Place the reserved mushroom liquid, stock, soy sauce, rice wine, spring onion and mushrooms in a saucepan and bring to the boil. Cook, covered, for 10 minutes.

4   Ladle the soup into the serving bowls and garnish with the coriander leaves.

INGREDIENTS

175 g (6 oz) dried thin egg noodles
2 tablespoons peanut oil
2 chicken breasts (about 250 g/9 oz each)
1 onion, sliced
1 small fresh red chilli, seeded and finely chopped
1 tablespoon finely chopped fresh ginger
2 tablespoons Indian curry powder
3 cups (750 ml/25 fl oz) chicken stock
800 ml (27 fl oz) coconut milk
300 g (10^{1}/$_{2}$ oz) baby bok choy, cut into long strips
^{1}/$_{3}$ cup (20 g/^{3}/$_{4}$ oz) fresh basil, torn

1 Cook the noodles in a large saucepan of boiling water for 3–4 minutes, or until cooked. Drain well and set aside. Wipe the saucepan clean and dry.

2 Heat the oil in the dry pan and add the chicken. Cook on each side for 5 minutes, or until cooked through. Remove the chicken and keep warm.

3 Place the onion in the pan and cook over low heat for 8 minutes, or until softened but not browned. Add the chilli, ginger and curry powder and cook for a further 2 minutes. Add the chicken stock and bring to the boil. Reduce the heat and simmer for 20 minutes. Thinly slice the chicken on the diagonal.

4 Add the coconut milk to the saucepan and simmer for 10 minutes. Add the bok choy and cook for 3 minutes, then stir in the basil.

5 To serve, divide the noodles among four deep serving bowls. Top with slices of chicken and ladle in the soup. Serve immediately.

INGREDIENTS

750 ml (3 cups) vegetable or chicken stock
250 g (9 oz) spinach and ricotta ravioli
85 g (3 oz) snowpeas (mangetout), sliced on the diagonal
2 tablespoons chopped flat-leaf (Italian) parsley
2 tablespoons chopped basil
grated Parmesan cheese, to garnish

1 Place the stock in a large heavy-based saucepan and bring to the boil. Add the ravioli and cook for 8–10 minutes, or until the pasta is al dente.

2 Season to taste with salt and pepper, and stir in the snowpeas, parsley and basil. Pour the soup into two bowls and sprinkle with grated Parmesan before serving.

INGREDIENTS

100 g ($^1/_2$ cup) dried haricot beans
125 g ($4^1/_2$ oz) bacon, cubed
40 g ($1^1/_2$ oz) butter
1 carrot, sliced
1 onion, chopped
1 leek, white part only, roughly chopped
1 turnip, peeled and chopped
bouquet garni
1.25 litres (5 cups) chicken stock
400 g (14 oz) white cabbage, finely shredded

1   Soak the beans overnight in cold water. Drain, put in a saucepan and cover with cold water. Bring to the boil and simmer for 5 minutes, then drain. Put the bacon in the same saucepan, cover with water and simmer for 5 minutes. Drain and pat dry with paper towels.

2   Melt the butter in a large heavy-based saucepan, add the bacon and cook for 5 minutes, without browning. Add the beans, carrot, onion, leek and turnip and cook for 5 minutes. Add the bouquet garni and chicken stock and bring to the boil. Cover and simmer for 30 minutes. Add the cabbage, uncover and simmer for 30 minutes, or until the beans are tender. Remove the bouquet garni before serving and season to taste.

CAPSICUM, SPINACH AND CHICKPEA SOUP

1 tablespoon olive oil
8 spring onions (scallions), finely sliced
1 red capsicum (pepper)
1 garlic clove, crushed
1 teaspoon cumin seeds
375 ml (1$\frac{1}{2}$ cups) Italian tomato passata
750 ml (3 cups) vegetable or beef stock
300 g (10$\frac{1}{2}$ oz) tin chickpeas, rinsed and drained
2 teaspoons red wine vinegar
1–2 teaspoons sugar
100 g (3$\frac{1}{2}$ oz) baby English spinach leaves

1 Heat the oil in a large heavy-based saucepan and stir in the spring onion. Reduce the heat and cook, covered, for 2–3 minutes, or until softened. Meanwhile, remove the seeds and membrane from the capsicum and finely dice. Add the capsicum, garlic and cumin seeds to the pan and cook for 1 minute.

2 Add the passata and stock and bring the mixture to the boil. Reduce the heat and simmer for 10 minutes. Add the chickpeas, vinegar and sugar to the soup and simmer for a further 5 minutes.

3 Stir in the baby spinach and season to taste with salt and ground black pepper. Cook until the spinach begins to wilt, then serve immediately.

INGREDIENTS

750 ml (3 cups) vegetable stock
1 tablespoon oil
1 onion, chopped
1 tablespoon grated fresh ginger
1 kg (2 lb 4 oz) carrots, chopped
2 tablespoons chopped coriander (cilantro) leaves

1   Place the stock in a pan and bring to the boil. Heat the oil in a large heavy-based pan,
    add the onion and ginger and cook for 2 minutes, or until the onion has softened.

2   Add the stock and carrots. Bring to the boil, then reduce the heat and simmer for
    10–15 minutes, or until the carrot is cooked and tender.

3   Place in a blender or food processor and process in batches until smooth. Return to the
    pan and add a little more stock or water to thin the soup to your preferred consistency.

4   Stir in the coriander and season to taste. Heat gently before serving.

CHICKPEA, POTATO AND SPINACH SOUP

INGREDIENTS

1 litre (4 cups) vegetable stock
1¹/₂ tablespoons olive oil
1 onion, finely chopped
1 large potato, cut into 1.5 cm (⁵/₈ inch) cubes
1¹/₂ teaspoons paprika
2 garlic cloves, crushed
400 g (14 oz) tin chickpeas, drained
1 large tomato, cut into small cubes
50 g (1 cup) English spinach, coarsely shredded
25 g (¹/₄ cup) grated Parmesan cheese

1   Place the stock in a saucepan, then cover and slowly bring to the boil. Heat the olive oil in a large heavy-based saucepan, and cook the onion for 2–3 minutes, or until soft.

2   Add the potato to the onion, and stir in the paprika, garlic and chickpeas. Add the onion mixture to the stock and bring to the boil. Stir in the tomato, and season with salt and cracked black pepper.

3   Simmer for 10 minutes, or until the potato is tender. Add the spinach and cook until wilted. Top with Parmesan, season to taste and serve.

1 loaf (200 g/7 oz) day-old white Italian bread, crust removed
155 g (1 cup) whole blanched almonds
3–4 garlic cloves, chopped
125 ml ($^1/_2$ cup) extra virgin olive oil
80 ml ($^1/_3$ cup) sherry or white wine vinegar
315–375 ml (1$^1/_4$–1$^1/_2$ cups) vegetable stock
2 tablespoons olive oil, extra
75 g (2$^1/_2$ oz) day-old white Italian bread, extra, crust removed, cut into 1 cm ($^1/_2$ inch) cubes
200 g (7 oz) small seedless green grapes

1 Soak the bread in cold water for 5 minutes, then squeeze out any excess liquid. Chop the almonds and garlic in a processor until well ground. Add the bread and process until the mixture is smooth.

2 With the motor running, add the olive oil in a steady slow stream until the mixture is the consistency of thick mayonnaise. Slowly add the sherry and 315 ml (1$^1/_4$ cups) of the stock. Blend for 1 minute. Season with salt. Refrigerate for at least 2 hours. The soup thickens on refrigeration so you may need to add extra stock or water to thin it.

3 When ready to serve, heat the extra oil in a frying pan, add the bread cubes and toss over medium heat for 2–3 minutes, or until golden. Drain on crumpled paper towels. Serve the soup very cold, garnished with the grapes and bread cubes.

CHILLED GARLIC AND ALMOND SOUP

INGREDIENTS

1 coriander (cilantro) sprig
4 cobs sweet corn
30 g (1 oz) butter
2 red capsicums (peppers), diced
1 small onion, finely chopped
1 small red chilli, finely chopped
1 tablespoon plain (all-purpose) flour
500 ml (2 cups) vegetable stock
125 ml ($^1/_2$ cup) cream

1   Trim the leaves off the coriander and finely chop the root and stems. Cut the kernels off the corn cobs.

2   Heat the butter in a saucepan over medium heat. Add the corn kernels, capsicum, onion and chilli and stir to coat in the butter. Cook, covered, over low heat, stirring occasionally, for 10 minutes, or until soft. Increase the heat to medium, add the coriander root and stem and cook, stirring, for 30 seconds, or until fragrant. Sprinkle with the flour and stir for 1 minute. Remove from the heat and gradually stir in the stock. Add 500 ml (2 cups) water and return to the heat. Bring to the boil, reduce the heat to low and simmer, covered, for 30 minutes, or until the vegetables are tender. Cool slightly.

3   Ladle 500 ml (2 cups) of the soup into a blender and purée until smooth. Return the purée to the soup in the pan, pour in the cream and gently heat until warmed through. Season. Sprinkle with the coriander leaves and serve. Delicious with grilled cheese on pitta bread.

4 red capsicums (peppers)

2 teaspoons oil

2 garlic cloves, crushed

4 spring onions (scallions), sliced

1 teaspoon finely chopped seeded chillies

425 g (15 oz) tin crushed tomatoes

125 ml ($^1/_2$ cup) chilled vegetable stock

1 teaspoon balsamic vinegar

2 tablespoons chopped basil

1 Cut the capsicums into quarters and remove the seeds and membrane. Place the capsicums skin-side up under a hot grill (broiler) and grill until the skins blacken and blister. Cool in a plastic bag, then peel away the skin and roughly chop the flesh.

2 Heat the oil in a small saucepan, add the garlic, spring onion and chilli, and cook over low heat for 1–2 minutes, or until softened.

3 Transfer to a food processor or blender, and add the capsicum, crushed tomatoes and stock. Blend until smooth, then stir in the vinegar and basil. Season to taste with salt and cracked pepper. Refrigerate, then serve cold.

INGREDIENTS

1 kg (2 lb) asparagus spears
30 g (1 oz) butter
1 onion, finely chopped
1 litre (4 cups) chicken stock
$1/4$ cup (7 g/$1/4$ oz) basil leaves, chopped
1 teaspoon celery salt
1 cup (250 ml/8 fl oz) cream

1 Break off woody ends from asparagus and trim off tips. Blanch the tips in boiling water for 1–2 minutes, refresh in cold water and set aside. Chop the remaining asparagus spears into large pieces.

2 Melt the butter in a large pan and cook the onion for 3–4 minutes over medium-low heat, or until soft and golden. Add the asparagus spears and cook for 1–2 minutes, stirring continuously.

3 Add chicken stock, basil and celery salt. Bring to the boil, reduce heat and simmer gently, covered, for 30 minutes.

4 Check that the asparagus is well cooked and soft. If not, simmer for a further 10 minutes. Set aside and allow to cool slightly.

5 Pour into a processor and process in batches until smooth. Sieve into a clean pan. Return to the heat, pour in cream and gently reheat. Do not allow the soup to boil. Season to taste with salt and pepper.

6 Serve immediately, with the asparagus tips placed on top of the soup.

30 g (1 oz) butter
2 large fennel bulbs, thinly sliced
2 leeks, thinly sliced
1 litre (4 cups) hot vegetable or chicken stock
2 rosemary sprigs
$1/_8$ teaspoon ground nutmeg
80 g ($1/_3$ cup) sour cream
25 g ($1/_4$ cup) finely grated Parmesan cheese
1 tablespoon oil
1 leek, extra, cut in half lengthways, and cut into 4 cm ($1^1/_2$ inch) lengths
grated Parmesan cheese, extra, to garnish
sour cream, extra, to garnish

1 Heat the butter in a large heavy-based saucepan, add the sliced fennel and leek, and cook, covered, over medium heat for 2–3 minutes, stirring occasionally.

2 Put the hot stock, rosemary sprigs and nutmeg in a saucepan and bring to the boil. Simmer over low heat for about 15 minutes, then remove the rosemary sprigs and add the fennel and leek mixture to the pan.

3 Transfer the soup to a blender or food processor and blend in batches until smooth. Return to the pan, and stir in the sour cream and Parmesan. Reheat over medium heat until hot. Season to taste with salt and cracked black pepper and keep warm.

4 Heat the oil in a frying pan and cook the extra leek for 2–3 minutes, or until soft but not browned.

5 Spoon the soup into six warm soup bowls and top with the fried leek. Garnish with the extra Parmesan and sour cream and serve immediately.

CREAM OF FENNEL AND LEEK SOUP

INGREDIENTS

1.25 kg (2¹/₂ lb) tomatoes
1 tablespoon oil
1 onion, chopped
1 clove garlic, chopped
1¹/₂ cups (375 ml/12 fl oz) chicken stock
2 tablespoons tomato paste (purée)
1 teaspoon sugar
1 cup (250 ml/8 fl oz) cream

1 Cut a cross in the base of each tomato. Cover with boiling water for 1 minute, plunge in iced water, drain and peel away the skins. Scoop out the seeds and discard, then roughly chop the flesh.

2 Heat the oil in a large pan and cook the onion for 3 minutes, or until soft. Add the garlic and cook for 1 minute longer. Add the tomato and cook for 5 minutes, stirring occasionally, until very soft. Stir in the stock, bring to the boil, reduce the heat and simmer for 10 minutes.

3 Cool slightly, then transfer to a food processor. Process in batches until smooth, and return to the pan. Add the tomato paste and sugar and bring to the boil, stirring continuously. Reduce the heat and stir in the cream but do not allow the soup to boil. Season to taste before serving. Serve with an extra spoonful of cream and chopped parsley, if you want.

INGREDIENTS

Paste
2 birds eye chillies, seeded and roughly chopped
2 stems lemon grass, white part only, roughly chopped
4 red Asian shallots, peeled
1 tablespoon roughly chopped fresh ginger
1 teaspoon ground turmeric
3 candlenuts, optional

110 g (4 oz) dried rice noodle sticks
1 tablespoon peanut oil
250 g (9 oz) butternut pumpkin (squash), cut into 2 cm
   (1 inch) chunks
800 ml (27 fl oz) coconut milk
600 g (21 oz) chicken breast fillets, cut into cubes
2 tablespoons lime juice
1 tablespoon fish sauce
1 cup (90 g/3 oz) bean sprouts
$^1/_2$ cup (15 g/$^1/_2$ oz) torn fresh basil
$^1/_2$ cup (10 g/$^1/_2$ oz) torn fresh mint
$^1/_2$ cup (50 g/1$^3/_4$ oz) unsalted peanuts, toasted and
   chopped
1 lime, cut into quarters

1 Place all the paste ingredients in a food processor with 1 tablespoon water and blend until smooth.

2 Soak the noodles in boiling water for 15–20 minutes. Drain.

3 Meanwhile, heat the oil in a wok and swirl to coat. Add the paste and stir over low heat for 5 minutes, or until aromatic. Add the pumpkin and coconut milk and simmer for 10 minutes. Add the chicken and simmer for 20 minutes. Stir in the lime juice and fish sauce.

4 Divide the noodles among four deep serving bowls, then ladle the soup over them. Garnish with the bean sprouts, basil, mint, peanuts and lime.

INGREDIENTS

30 g (1 oz) butter
1½ tablespoons olive oil
1 leek, white part only, sliced
1 fennel bulb, sliced
375 g (12 oz) asparagus, cut into pieces
1 clove garlic, crushed
8 mint leaves, chopped
150 g (5 oz) shelled or frozen peas (400 g/13 oz in pods)
200 g (6½ oz) potatoes, cubed
4 cups (1 litre) chicken or vegetable stock
pinch of cayenne pepper
pinch of ground nutmeg

Mint and garlic croutons
20 g (¾ oz) butter
1 tablespoon olive oil
2 slices day-old white bread, crusts removed, cut into four
   mint leaves
2 cloves garlic, sliced, soaked in cold water

1   Heat the butter and oil in a large pan and add the leek and fennel. Cook over medium heat for 8–10 minutes, then stir in the asparagus, garlic, mint, peas and potato. Cook for 1 minute longer.

2   Add enough stock to cover the vegetables, and bring to the boil. Remove 4 asparagus tips, plunge into a bowl of iced water and set aside. Reduce the heat and simmer for 15–20 minutes, or until the vegetables are tender. Cool slightly then purée in a food processor. Return to the pan with the remaining stock, cayenne pepper and nutmeg and season.

3   Preheat the oven to moderately hot 190°C (375°F/Gas 5). To make the croutons, melt the butter and oil and brush on both sides of the bread. Lay on a baking tray. Tear the mint leaves in half, and place on the bread; dry the garlic and place on the mint. Drizzle the remaining butter mixture over the top. Bake for 5–6 minutes, or until the bread is toasted and the garlic golden.

4   Gently reheat the soup and serve garnished with the croutons and the reserved asparagus tips.

2 tablespoons butter
100 g (about 4) French shallots, roughly chopped
3 garlic cloves, crushed
30 g (1 cup) firmly packed flat-leaf (Italian) parsley
315 ml (1^1/$_4$ cups) vegetable or chicken stock
315 ml (1^1/$_4$ cups) milk
600 g (1 lb 5 oz) button mushrooms
^{1}/$_4$ teaspoon ground nutmeg
^{1}/$_4$ teaspoon cayenne pepper
150 g (5^1/$_2$ oz) light sour cream
cayenne pepper, to garnish

1 Melt the butter in a large heavy-based saucepan and add the shallots, garlic and parsley. Cook over medium heat for 2–3 minutes. Put the stock and milk in a separate saucepan and bring to the boil.

2 Gently wipe the mushrooms, then chop and add to the shallot mixture. Season with salt and pepper, and stir in the nutmeg and cayenne pepper. Cook, stirring, for 1 minute. Add the stock and milk, bring to the boil, then reduce the heat and simmer for 5 minutes. Transfer the soup to a blender or food processor and blend until smooth. Return to the pan.

3 Stir in the sour cream, adjust the seasoning and reheat gently. Serve sprinkled with cayenne pepper.

FRESH MUSHROOM, SHALLOT AND SOUR CREAM SOUP

GAZPACHO

750 g (1$^1/_2$ lb) ripe tomatoes

1 Lebanese cucumber, chopped

1 green capsicum (pepper), chopped

2–3 cloves garlic, crushed

1–2 tablespoons finely chopped black olives (optional)

$^1/_3$ cup (80 ml/2$^3/_4$ fl oz) red or white wine vinegar

$^1/_4$ cup (60 ml/2 fl oz) olive oil

1 tablespoon tomato paste (purée)

Accompaniments

1 onion, finely chopped

1 red capsicum (pepper), finely chopped

2 spring onions, finely chopped

1 Lebanese cucumber, finely chopped

2 hard-boiled eggs, chopped

chopped mint or parsley

Garlic and herb croutons

1 Score a cross in the base of each tomato. Cover with boiling water for 1 minute, plunge into cold water, drain and peel away the skins. Chop the flesh so finely that it is almost a purée.

2 Mix together the tomato, cucumber, capsicum, garlic, olives, vinegar, oil, and tomato paste, and season to taste. Cover and refrigerate for 2–3 hours.

3 Use 2–3 cups (750 ml/24 fl oz) of chilled water to thin the soup to your taste. Serve chilled, with the chopped onion, capsicum, spring onion, cucumber, boiled egg, herbs and croutons served separately for diners to add to their own bowls.

INGREDIENTS

tablespoons olive oil
onions, chopped
ashers bacon, chopped
potato, chopped into large cubes
280 g (9 oz) sweet potato (kumera) , chopped into large cubes
carrots, sliced
250 g (8 oz) pumpkin, cubed
400 g (13 oz) cabbage, shredded
280 g (9 oz) yellow squash, sliced
220 g (7 oz) green beans, chopped
2 x 400 g (13 oz) can chopped tomatoes
6 cups (1.5 litres) chicken stock
1 teaspoon dried Italian herbs
1 teaspoon dried oregano
½ cup (80 g/2³/₄ oz) macaroni
300 g (10 oz) can butter beans
grated Parmesan, to serve

1 Heat the oil and cook the onion and bacon for 3–4 minutes over moderate heat, or until the onion is just brown. Reduce the heat slightly and add the potato and sweet potato. Stir and cook for 1-2 minutes. Add the carrot and pumpkin and cook for a further 1–2 minutes, stirring continuously.

2 Add the cabbage, squash, green beans, tomato, stock and herbs. Increase the heat and bring to the boil. Reduce the heat and simmer gently, cover, for 1 hour.

3 Add the macaroni and butter beans and cook for a further 10–12 minutes, or until the pasta is tender. Season to taste. Serve with Parmesan.

JERUSALEM ARTICHOKE AND ROAST GARLIC SOUP

INGREDIENTS

1 garlic head
2 tablespoons butter
1 tablespoon olive oil
1 onion, chopped
1 leek, white part only, washed and chopped
1 celery stalk, chopped
700 g (1 lb 9 oz) Jerusalem artichokes, peeled and chopped
1 small potato, chopped
1.5 litres (6 cups) vegetable or chicken stock
olive oil, to serve
finely chopped chives, to serve

1 Preheat the oven to 200°C (400°F/Gas 6). Slice the base from the head of garlic, wrap it in foil and roast for 30 minutes, or until soft. When cool enough to handle, remove from the foil and slip the cloves from the skin. Set aside.

2 In a large heavy-based saucepan, heat the butter and oil. Add the onion, leek and celery and a large pinch of salt, and cook for 10 minutes, or until soft. Add the Jerusalem artichokes, potato and garlic and cook for a further 10 minutes. Pour in the stock, bring the mixture to the boil, then reduce the heat and simmer for 30 minutes, or until the vegetables are soft.

3 Purée in a blender until smooth, and season well. Serve with a drizzle of olive oil and some chives. Delicious with warm crusty bread.

INGREDIENTS

80 g ($^1/_2$ cup) macaroni
1 tablespoon olive oil
1 leek, sliced
2 garlic cloves, crushed
1 carrot, sliced
1 waxy potato, chopped
1 zucchini (courgette), sliced
2 celery stalks, sliced
100 g (3$^1/_2$ oz) green beans, cut into short lengths
425 g (15 oz) tin chopped tomatoes
2 litres (8 cups) vegetable or beef stock
2 tablespoons tomato paste (purée)
425 g (15 oz) tin cannellini beans, rinsed and drained
2 tablespoons chopped flat-leaf (Italian) parsley
shaved Parmesan cheese, to serve

1   Bring a saucepan of water to the boil, add the macaroni and cook for 10–12 minutes, or until tender. Drain.

2   Meanwhile, heat the oil in a large heavy-based saucepan, add the leek and garlic and cook over medium heat for 3–4 minutes.

3   Add the carrot, potato, zucchini, celery, green beans, tomato, stock and tomato paste. Bring to the boil, then reduce the heat and simmer for 10 minutes, or until the vegetables are tender.

4   Stir in the cooked pasta and cannellini beans and heat through. Spoon into warmed serving bowls and garnish with parsley and shaved Parmesan.

INGREDIENTS

400 g (14 oz) field mushrooms
60 g (2'/₄ oz) butter
1 small onion, finely chopped
1 garlic clove, crushed
30 g ('/₄ cup) plain (all-purpose) flour
750 ml (3 cups) chicken stock
2 tablespoons fresh thyme leaves
2 tablespoons sherry
250 ml (1 cup) cream
1 sheet frozen puff pastry, thawed
1 egg, lightly beaten

1   Preheat the oven to 200°C (400°F/Gas 6). Roughly chop the mushrooms. Melt the butter in a pan and cook the onion for 3 minutes, until soft. Add the garlic; cook for 1 minute. Add the mushrooms; cook until soft. Sprinkle with the flour and stir for 1 minute.

2   Stir in the stock, add the thyme and bring to the boil. Reduce the heat, cover and simmer for 10 minutes. Cool and process in batches. Return to the pan, stir in the sherry and cream and pour into four ovenproof bowls.

3   Cut rounds of pastry slightly larger than the bowl tops and cover each bowl with pastry (use small deep bowls rather than wide shallow ones or the pastry may sag into the soup).

4   Seal the pastry edges and brush lightly with the beaten egg. Bake for 15 minutes, until golden and puffed.

INGREDIENTS

250 g (9 oz) dried soba noodles
8 raw prawns (shrimp)
1¹/₂ tablespoons finely chopped ginger
4 spring onions (scallions), cut on the diagonal
100 ml (3¹/₂ fl oz) light soy sauce
60 ml (¹/₄ cup) mirin
1 teaspoon grated palm sugar or soft brown sugar
300 g (10¹/₂ oz) boneless salmon fillet, skinned and cut into 5 cm (2 in) strips
300 g (10¹/₂ oz) boneless white fish fillet, skinned and cut into 5 cm (2 in) strips
150 g (5¹/₂ oz) cleaned calamari hood, scored and cut into 3 cm (1¹/₄ in) cubes
50 g (1³/₄ oz) mizuna, roughly chopped (see note)

1 Cook the noodles in a large saucepan of boiling water for 5 minutes, or until they are tender. Drain and rinse with cold water.

2 Peel and devein the prawns, reserving the shells and leaving the tails intact. Place the heads and shells in a large saucepan with the ginger, half the spring onion and 1.5 litres (6 cups) water. Bring slowly to the boil and boil for 5 minutes. Strain and discard the prawn heads, shells and spring onion. Return the stock to the pan. Add the soy sauce, mirin and palm sugar to the stock. Heat and stir to dissolve the sugar.

3 Add the seafood to the pan and poach over low heat for 2–3 minutes, or until it is just cooked. Add the remaining spring onion.

4 Divide the noodles evenly among four large bowls. Add the seafood, pour on the stock and scatter with the mizuna.

NOTE Mizuna is a salad leaf with dark green, feathery and glossy leaves. It has a mild peppery flavour. Young leaves are often used in salads or as a garnish, while older leaves are used in stir-fries or in Japanese cooking.

POTATO AND ROCKET SOUP

INGREDIENTS

1.5 litres (6 cups) vegetable or chicken stock
1.25 kg (2 lb 12 oz) desiree potatoes, chopped into small pieces
2 large garlic cloves, peeled, left whole
250 g (9 oz) rocket (arugula)
1 tablespoon extra virgin olive oil
extra rocket (arugula) leaves, to garnish (optional)
50 g (¹/₂ cup) shaved Parmesan cheese

1   Place the stock in a large heavy-based saucepan and bring to the boil. Add the potato and garlic and simmer over medium heat for 15 minutes, or until the potato is tender to the point of a sharp knife. Add the rocket and simmer for a further 2 minutes. Stir in the olive oil.

2   Transfer the mixture to a blender or food processor and blend in batches until smooth. Return the mixture to the pan and stir over medium heat until hot. Season to taste with salt and cracked black pepper and serve in warmed bowls. Garnish with the rocket leaves and shaved Parmesan before serving.

6 cobs sweet corn
2 tablespoons vegetable oil
1 onion, finely diced
3 garlic cloves, crushed
1 celery stalk, diced
1 carrot, peeled and diced
2 large potatoes, peeled and diced
1 litre (4 cups) vegetable or chicken stock
2 tablespoons finely chopped flat-leaf (Italian) parsley

1 Bring a large pot of salted water to the boil, and cook the sweet corn for 5 minutes.
Reserve 250 ml (1 cup) of the cooking water. Cut the corn kernels from the cob, place
half in a blender with the reserved cooking water, and blend until smooth.

2 Heat the oil in a large saucepan, add the onion, garlic, celery and a large pinch of salt and
cook for 5 minutes. Add the carrot and potatoes, cook for a further 5 minutes, then add
the stock, corn kernels and blended corn mixture. Reduce the heat and simmer for
20 minutes, or until the vegetables are tender. Season well, and stir in the chopped parsley
before serving.

POTATO AND SWEET CORN CHOWDER

INGREDIENTS

500 ml (2 cups) vegetable stock
750 g (1 ib 10 oz) butternut pumpkin (squash), cut into 1.5 cm ($^5/_8$ inch) cubes
2 onions, chopped
2 garlic cloves, halved
$^1/_4$ teaspoon ground nutmeg
60 ml ($^1/_4$ cup) cream

1   Put the stock and 500 ml (2 cups) water in a large heavy-based saucepan and bring to
    the boil. Add the pumpkin, onion and garlic and return to the boil. Reduce the heat slightly
    and cook for 15 minutes, or until the pumpkin is soft.

2   Drain the vegetables through a colander, reserving the liquid. Purée the pumpkin mixture
    in a blender until smooth (you may need to add some of the reserved liquid). Return the
    pumpkin purée to the pan and stir in enough of the reserved liquid to reach the desired
    consistency. Season to taste with nutmeg, salt and cracked black pepper.

3   Ladle the soup into four soup bowls and pour some cream into each bowl to create a swirl
    pattern on the top. Serve with warm crusty bread.

2 tablespoons olive oil

1 large red onion, finely chopped

2 garlic cloves, crushed

2 tablespoons tomato paste (purée)

2 tomatoes, finely chopped

2 teaspoons paprika

1 teaspoon cayenne pepper

500 g (2 cups) red lentils

50 g ($^1/_4$ cup) long-grain rice

2.125 litres (8$^1/_2$ cups) chicken stock

45 g ($^1/_4$ cup) fine burghul (bulgar wheat)

2 tablespoons chopped mint

2 tablespoons chopped flat-leaf (Italian) parsley

90 g ($^1/_3$ cup) thick natural yoghurt

$^1/_4$ preserved lemon, pulp removed, zest washed and julienned

1 Heat the oil in a saucepan over medium heat. Add the onion and garlic and cook for 2–3 minutes, or until soft. Stir in the tomato paste, tomato and spices and cook for 1 minute.

2 Add the lentils, rice and chicken stock, then cover and bring to the boil over high heat. Reduce the heat and simmer for 30–35 minutes, or until the rice is cooked.

3 Stir in the burghul and herbs, then season to taste. Divide the soup among serving bowls, garnish with yoghurt and preserved lemon and serve immediately.

NOTE This soup will thicken on standing, so if reheating you may need to add more liquid.

RED LENTIL, BURGHUL AND MINT SOUP

INGREDIENTS

1 tablespoon olive oil
20 g ($^3/_4$ oz) butter
2 rashers bacon, chopped
3 leeks, chopped
2 cloves garlic, chopped
1 stick celery, coarsely chopped
2 zucchini, coarsely chopped
2 bay leaves
6 cups (1.5 litres) chicken stock
$^1/_3$ cup (80 ml/$2^3/_4$ fl oz) cream
$^1/_4$ cup (15 g/$^1/_2$ oz) finely chopped parsley
2 rashers bacon, extra, to serve

1 Preheat the oven to warm 160°C (315°F/Gas 2–3). Heat the oil and butter in a large roasting tin. Add the bacon rashers and stir over medium heat for 1–2 minutes. Add the leek, garlic, celery, zucchini and bay leaves and cook, stirring, for 2–3 minutes, without allowing to brown.

2 Transfer the roasting tin to the oven and roast the vegetables and bacon for 40 minutes, turning a couple of times. Cover with foil if starting to brown. Transfer to a large pan, pour on the stock and bring to the boil. Lower the heat and simmer for 30 minutes. Cool slightly, strain and return the liquid to the pan. Remove the bay leaves.

3 Put the vegetables and bacon in a food processor with a ladleful of the cooking liquid and process until smooth, adding more liquid if necessary. Return the purée to the pan with the liquid and add some pepper, the cream and parsley. Reheat gently.

4 To make the bacon garnish, trim off the rind and excess fat from the bacon and grill until crisp. Drain on paper towels, then crumble with your fingers and serve on top of the soup.

2 carrots, cut into large pieces
1 parsnip, cut into large pieces
500 g (1 lb) unpeeled pumpkin, cut into large pieces
350 g (11 oz) unpeeled sweet potato, cut into large pieces
1 red capsicum, cut into large pieces
2 onions, halved
4 cloves garlic, unpeeled
3 cups (750 ml/24 fl oz) vegetable stock
sour cream and thyme, to serve

1 Preheat the oven to moderate 180°C (350°F/Gas 4). Put the vegetables in a large greased baking dish and brush lightly with some olive oil.

2 Bake for 1 hour, turning often. Remove the capsicum. Bake for 30 minutes longer; cool the vegetables slightly. Remove the skin from the capsicum; place in a food processor with the carrot, parsnip and onion.

3 Scrape the pumpkin and sweet potato flesh into the processor and squeeze in the garlic pulp. Add half the stock and purée until smooth. Place in a pan with the remaining stock and heat through. Season and serve with sour cream and thyme.

ROASTED VEGETABLE SOUP

INGREDIENTS

1 pinch saffron threads
250 g (9 oz) Jerusalem artichokes
2 tablespoons lemon juice
1 tablespoon olive oil
1 large onion, finely chopped
1 litre (4 cups) vegetable or chicken stock
3 teaspoons ground cumin
500 g (1 lb 2 oz) desiree potatoes, grated
2 teaspoons lemon juice, extra

1   Place the saffron threads in a bowl with 2 tablespoons boiling water and leave until needed. Peel and thinly slice the artichokes, dropping the slices into a bowl of water mixed with lemon juice to prevent discolouration.

2   Heat the oil in a large heavy-based saucepan, add the onion and cook over medium heat for 2–3 minutes, or until the onion is softened. Bring the stock to the boil in a separate saucepan. Add the cumin to the onion mixture and cook for a further 30 seconds, or until fragrant. Add the drained artichokes, potato, saffron mixture, stock and extra lemon juice. Bring to the boil, then reduce the heat and simmer for 15–18 minutes, or until the artichokes are very soft.

3   Transfer to a blender and process in batches until smooth. Return the soup to the pan and season to taste with salt and cracked pepper. Reheat over medium heat and serve.

INGREDIENTS

30 g (1 oz) butter
1 large onion, finely chopped
1 garlic clove, crushed
2 litres (8 cups) vegetable or chicken stock
200 g (1 cup) risoni
$^1/_2$ baguette, cut into 6 slices
15 g ($^1/_2$ oz) butter, extra, melted
1 teaspoon Dijon mustard
50 g (1$^3/_4$ oz) Gruyère cheese, coarsely grated
500 g (1 lb 2 oz) silverbeet (Swiss chard), central stalk removed, shredded
30 g (1 cup) basil, torn

1   Heat the butter in a large heavy-based saucepan, add the onion and garlic and cook over medium heat for 2–3 minutes, or until the onion is softened. Meanwhile, place the stock in a separate pan and bring to the boil.

2   Add the stock to the onion mixture and bring to the boil. Add the risoni, reduce the heat and simmer for 8 minutes, stirring occasionally.

3   Meanwhile, place the baguette slices in a single layer on a baking tray and cook under a preheated grill (broiler) until golden brown on one side. Turn the slices over and brush with the combined melted butter and mustard. Top with the Gruyère and grill until the cheese has melted.

4   Add the silverbeet and basil to the risoni mixture and simmer for about 1 minute, or until the risoni is al dente and the silverbeet is cooked. Season with salt and freshly ground black pepper and serve with the Gruyère croutons.

INGREDIENTS

1 tablespoon peanut or vegetable oil
1 onion, chopped
2 garlic cloves, chopped
1$^{1}/_{2}$ teaspoons chopped fresh ginger
1$^{1}/_{2}$ tablespoons Madras curry paste
100 g (3$^{1}/_{2}$ oz) yellow split peas, rinsed and drained1 large zucchini (courgette), peeled and chopped
1 large carrot, roughly chopped
170 g (6 oz) button mushrooms, roughly chopped
1 celery stalk, roughly chopped
1 litre (4 cups) vegetable stock
125 ml ($^{1}/_{2}$ cup) cream

1   Heat the oil in a saucepan, add the onion and cook over low heat for 5 minutes, or until soft. Add the garlic, ginger and curry paste and cook over medium heat for 2 minutes. Stir in the split peas until well coated with paste, then add the zucchini, carrot, mushroom and celery and cook for 2 minutes.

2   Add the stock, bring to the boil, then reduce the heat and simmer, partly covered, for 1 hour. Remove from the heat and allow to cool slightly.

3   Transfer the soup to a blender or food processor and process in batches until smooth. Return to the pan, stir in the cream and gently heat until warmed through. Delicious served with naan bread.

1 tablespoon oil
1 onion, chopped
2 garlic cloves, finely chopped
1–2 small red chillies, finely chopped
$^1/_4$ teaspoon paprika
750 g (1 lb 10 oz) orange sweet potato (kumera), chopped into small pieces
1 litre (4 cups) vegetable or beef stock
chopped dried chilli, to garnish

1 Heat the oil in a large heavy-based saucepan, add the onion and cook for 1–2 minutes, or until soft. Add the garlic, chilli and paprika and cook for a further 2 minutes, or until aromatic. Add the sweet potato to the pan and toss to coat with the spices.

2 Pour in the stock, bring to the boil, then reduce the heat and simmer for 15 minutes, or until the vegetables are tender. Cool slightly, then transfer to a blender or food processor and blend in batches until smooth, adding extra water if needed to reach the desired consistency. Do not overblend or the mixture may become gluey.

3 Season to taste with salt and black pepper. Ladle the soup into bowls, sprinkle with dried chilli and serve.

INGREDIENTS

25 g (1 oz) butter
1 small white onion, finely chopped
750 g (1 lb 10 oz) orange sweet potato, peeled and cut into 2 cm ($^3/_4$ inch) dice
2 firm pears (500 g/1 lb 2 oz), peeled, cored and cut into 2 cm ($^3/_4$ inch) dice
750 ml (3 cups) vegetable or chicken stock
250 ml (1 cup) cream
mint leaves, to garnish

1 Melt the butter in a saucepan over medium heat, add the onion and cook for 2–3 minutes, or until softened but not brown. Add the sweet potato and pear, and cook, stirring, for 1–2 minutes. Add the stock to the pan, bring to the boil and cook for 20 minutes, or until the sweet potato and pear are soft.

2 Cool slightly, then place the mixture in a blender or food processor and blend in batches until smooth. Return to the pan, stir in the cream and gently reheat without boiling. Season with salt and ground black pepper. Garnish with the mint.

INGREDIENTS

750 g (1 lb 10 oz) vine-ripened tomatoes
1 loaf (450 g/1 lb) day-old crusty Italian bread
1 tablespoon olive oil
3 garlic cloves, crushed
1 tablespoon tomato paste (purée)
1.25 litres (5 cups) hot vegetable stock
4 tablespoons torn basil leaves
2–3 tablespoons extra virgin olive oil, plus extra, to serve

1 Score a cross in the base of each tomato. Place in a bowl of boiling water for 1 minute, then plunge into cold water and peel the skin away from the cross. Cut the tomatoes in half and scoop out the seeds with a teaspoon. Chop the tomato flesh.

2 Remove most of the crust from the bread and discard. Cut the bread into 3 cm (1¼ in) pieces.

3 Heat the oil in a large saucepan. Add the garlic, tomato and tomato paste, then reduce the heat and simmer, stirring occasionally, for 15 minutes until thickened. Add the stock and bring to the boil, stirring for 2 minutes. Reduce the heat to medium, add the bread pieces and cook, stirring, for 5 minutes, or until the bread softens and absorbs most of the liquid. Add more stock or water if necessary.

4 Stir in the torn basil leaves and extra virgin olive oil, and leave for 5 minutes so the flavours have time to develop. Drizzle with a little of the extra oil.

NOTE This soup is popular in Italy in the summer months when tomatoes are at their tastiest, and as a way of using up leftover bread. In Italy, the soup is called Pappa al pomodoro.

INGREDIENTS

2 tablespoons vegetable oil

2 tablespoons olive oil

2 red onions, finely chopped

2 garlic cloves, crushed

1 tablespoon ground cumin

$1/4$ teaspoon ground cayenne pepper

2 teaspoons paprika

2 red capsicums (peppers), diced

90 g ($1/3$ cup) tomato paste (purée)

250 ml (1 cup) dry white wine

2 x 400 g (14 oz) cans chopped tomatoes

2 long red chillies, seeded and chopped

500 ml (2 cups) chicken or vegetable stock

3 tablespoons chopped flat-leaf (Italian) parsley

4 tablespoons chopped coriander (cilantro) leaves

Polenta and olive sticks

500 ml (2 cups) chicken or vegetable stock

185 g ($1\frac{1}{4}$ cups) coarse polenta (cornmeal)

100 g ($3\frac{1}{2}$ oz) pitted Kalamata olives, chopped

125 ml ($1/2$ cup) olive oil, to deep-fry

1 Heat the oils in a large saucepan over medium heat and cook the onion and garlic for 2–3 minutes, or until soft.

2 Reduce the heat to low, add the spices and cook for 1–2 minutes. Add the capsicum and cook for 5 minutes. Stir in the tomato paste and wine, simmer for 2 minutes, or until reduced slightly. Add the tomato, chilli, stock and 500 ml (2 cups) water. Season. Simmer for 20 minutes. Purée the soup with the herbs.

3 To make the polenta and olive sticks, grease a 20 cm x 30 cm (8 inch x 12 inch) baking tray. Bring the stock and 500 ml (2 cups) water to the boil in a saucepan. Slowly add the polenta in a fine stream, whisking until smooth. Reduce the heat to low. Cook, stirring constantly, for 15–20 minutes, or until it starts to come away from the side. Stir in the olives, then spoon into the tray, smoothing the surface. Cover and chill for 30 minutes, or until firm. Cut into sticks.

4 Heat the oil in a large deep frying pan to 190°C (375°F), or until a cube of bread browns in 10 seconds. Cook the sticks in batches on each side for 1–2 minutes, or until crisp. Drain well, and serve with the soup.

INGREDIENTS

2 tablespoons olive oil

1 small leek, white part only, chopped

2 garlic cloves, crushed

2 teaspoons curry powder

1 teaspoon ground cumin

1 teaspoon garam masala

1 litre (4 cups) vegetable stock

1 bay leaf

185 g (1 cup) brown lentils

450 g (1 lb) butternut pumpkin (squash), peeled and cut into
    1 cm ($^1/_2$ inch) cubes

2 zucchini (courgettes), cut in half lengthways and sliced

400 g (14 oz) tin chopped tomatoes

200 g (7 oz) broccoli, cut into small florets

1 small carrot, diced

80 g ($^1/_2$ cup) peas

1 tablespoon chopped mint

Spiced yoghurt

250 g (1 cup) thick plain yoghurt

1 tablespoon chopped coriander (cilantro) leaves

1 garlic clove, crushed

3 dashes Tabasco sauce

1 Heat the oil in a saucepan over medium heat. Add the leek and garlic and cook for 4–5 minutes, or until soft and lightly golden. Add the curry powder, cumin and garam masala and cook for 1 minute, or until fragrant.

2 Add the stock, bay leaf, lentils and pumpkin. Bring to the boil, then reduce the heat to low and simmer for 10–15 minutes, or until the lentils are tender. Season well.

3 Add the zucchini, tomatoes, broccoli, carrot and 500 ml (2 cups) water and simmer for 10 minutes, or until the vegetables are tender. Add the peas and simmer for 2–3 minutes.

4 To make the spiced yoghurt, place the yoghurt, coriander, garlic and Tabasco in a small bowl and stir until combined.

5 Dollop a spoonful of the yoghurt on each serving of soup and garnish with the chopped mint.

INGREDIENTS

2 teaspoons olive oil
1 onion, chopped
1 carrot, chopped
2 celery sticks, chopped
350 g (11 oz) sweet potato (kumera), chopped
400 g (13 oz) can corn kernels, drained
1 litre vegetable stock
1 cup (90 g/3 oz) pasta spirals

1   Heat the oil in a large pan and add the onion, carrot and celery. Cook the vegetables over low heat, stirring regularly, for 10 minutes, or until they are soft.

2   Add the sweet potato, corn kernels and stock. Bring to the boil and then reduce the heat and simmer for 20 minutes, or until the vegetables are tender.

3   Add the pasta to the pan and return to the boil. Reduce the heat and simmer for 10 minutes, or until the pasta is tender. Season the soup and serve immediately.

INGREDIENTS

1 tablespoon olive oil
1 large onion, finely chopped
2 garlic cloves, crushed
750 ml (3 cups) vegetable or chicken stock
750 g (1 lb 10 oz) zucchini (courgettes), thinly sliced
60 ml ($^1/_4$ cup) cream
toasted ciabatta bread, to serve

Pesto
50 g (1 cup) basil
25 g ($^1/_4$ cup) finely grated Parmesan cheese
2 tablespoons pine nuts, toasted
2 tablespoons extra virgin olive oil

1   Heat the oil in a large heavy-based saucepan. Add the onion and garlic and cook over medium heat for 5 minutes, or until the onion is soft.

2   Bring the stock to the boil in a separate saucepan. Add the zucchini and hot stock to the onion mixture. Bring to the boil, then reduce the heat, cover and simmer for about 10 minutes, or until the zucchini is very soft.

3   To make the pesto, process the basil, Parmesan and pine nuts in a food processor for 20 seconds, or until finely chopped. Gradually add the olive oil and process until smooth. Spoon into a small bowl.

4   Transfer the zucchini mixture to a blender or food processor and blend in batches until smooth. Return the mixture to the pan, stir in the cream and 2 tablespoons of the pesto, and reheat over medium heat until hot. Season with salt and black pepper and serve with toasted ciabatta bread. Serve the remaining pesto in a bowl for diners to help themselves, or cover with olive oil and store in the refrigerator for up to 1 week.

INGREDIENTS

2 x 400 g (14 oz) tins cannellini beans
1 tablespoon extra virgin olive oil
1 leek, finely chopped
2 garlic cloves, crushed
1 teaspoon thyme leaves
2 celery stalks, diced
1 carrot, diced
1 kg (2 lb 4 oz) silverbeet (Swiss chard), trimmed and roughly chopped
1 ripe tomato, diced
1 litre (4 cups) vegetable stock
2 small crusty rolls, each cut into 4 slices
2 teaspoons balsamic vinegar
35 g (1/3 cup) finely grated Parmesan cheese

1 Put one tin of beans and liquid in a blender or small food processor and blend until smooth. Drain the other tin, reserving the beans and discarding the liquid.

2 Heat the oil in a large heavy-based saucepan, add the leek, garlic and thyme and cook for 2–3 minutes, or until soft and aromatic. Add the celery, carrot, silverbeet and tomato and cook for a further 2–3 minutes, or until the silverbeet has wilted. Heat the stock in a separate saucepan.

3 Stir the puréed cannellini beans and stock into the vegetable mixture. Bring to the boil, then reduce the heat and simmer for 5–10 minutes, or until the vegetables are tender. Add the drained beans and stir until heated through. Season to taste with salt and cracked black pepper.

4 Arrange 2 slices of bread in the base of each soup bowl. Stir the balsamic vinegar into the soup and ladle over the bread. Serve topped with grated Parmesan.

NOTE This recipe is the authentic bean soup from Florence. If you like, spice it up by adding chopped chilli.

INGREDIENTS

1 carrot, chopped
1 large leek, chopped
2 bay leaves
2 chicken breast fillets
2 litres (8 cups) chicken stock
75 g ($\frac{1}{3}$ cup) short-grain rice
3 eggs, separated
80 ml ($\frac{1}{3}$ cup) lemon juice
2 tablespoons chopped parsley
40 g ($1\frac{1}{2}$ oz) butter, chopped

1   Place the carrot, leek, bay leaves, chicken fillets and stock in a large saucepan. Bring to the boil over high heat, then reduce the heat and simmer for 10–15 minutes, or until the chicken is cooked. Strain into a clean saucepan and reserve the chicken.

2   Add the rice to the liquid, bring to the boil, then reduce the heat and simmer for 15 minutes, or until tender. Cut the chicken into 1 cm ($\frac{1}{2}$ in) cubes.

3   Whisk the egg whites in a clean, dry bowl until firm peaks form. Beat in the yolks until light and creamy, whisk in the lemon juice, then 250 ml (1 cup) of the soup. Remove the soup from the heat and gradually whisk in the egg mixture. Add the chicken and stir over low heat for 2 minutes — do not boil or the egg will scramble. Serve at once with a sprinkle of parsley and dot of butter.

NOTE   This soup will not stand well — make just before serving.

INGREDIENTS

1 kg (2 lb) gravy beef, cut into small pieces
500 g (1 lb) beef bones including marrow, cut into small pieces (ask your butcher to do this)
1 leek, cut into small pieces
2 onions, quartered
2 carrots, chopped
2 sticks celery, chopped
6 black peppercorns
6 whole cloves
3 sprigs thyme
3 sprigs parsley
3 bay leaves
1 egg shell, crumbled
1 egg white, lightly beaten
2 tablespoons chopped parsley

1 Preheat the oven to moderate 180°C (350°F/Gas 4). Place the gravy beef and beef bones in a single layer in a baking dish. Bake for 45 minutes, or until lightly browned, turning once.

2 Put the meat, bones, vegetables, peppercorns, cloves, herbs, bay leaves and 1 teaspoon of salt in a large pan. Add 3 litres of water and slowly bring to the boil. Reduce the heat to low, cover and simmer for 4 hours. Set aside to cool slightly. Remove the larger pieces of meat and discard. Ladle the liquid through a muslin-lined sieve into a bowl. Discard the remaining meat and vegetables.

3 Cover the liquid and refrigerate for several hours, or overnight. Spoon off the fat from the surface. Return to a clean pan with the egg shell and the lightly beaten egg white.

4 Slowly heat the stock to simmering and simmer for 10 minutes. A frothy scum will form on the surface. Remove from the heat and leave for 10 minutes. Skim the surface and ladle the stock through a muslin-lined sieve. Reheat, season if needed, and serve with the chopped parsley.

INGREDIENTS

200 g (7 oz) rice noodle sticks
1.5 litres (6 cups) beef stock
1 star anise
4 cm (1$^1/_2$ in) piece fresh ginger, sliced
2 pigs trotters (ask your butcher to cut them in half)
$^1/_2$ onion, studded with 2 cloves
2 stems lemon grass, pounded
2 garlic cloves, pounded
$^1/_4$ teaspoon white pepper
1 tablespoon fish sauce
400 g (14 oz) beef fillet, partially frozen, and thinly sliced
90 g (1 cup) bean sprouts
2 spring onions (scallions), thinly sliced on the diagonal
25 g ($^1/_2$ cup) fresh coriander (cilantro) leaves, chopped
25 g ($^1/_2$ cup) fresh Vietnamese mint, chopped
1 fresh red chilli, thinly sliced
fresh red chillies, extra, to serve
fresh Vietnamese mint, extra, to serve
fresh coriander (cilantro) leaves, extra, to serve
2 limes, cut into quarters
fish sauce, extra, to serve

1   Soak the noodles in boiling water for 15–20 minutes. Drain.

2   Bring the stock, star anise, ginger, trotters, onion, lemon grass, garlic and white pepper to
the boil in a large saucepan. Reduce the heat and simmer for 30 minutes. Strain, return to
the same pan and stir in the fish sauce.

3   Divide the noodles among bowls, then top with beef strips, sprouts, spring onion,
coriander, mint and chilli. Ladle on the broth.

4   Place the extra chilli, mint, coriander, lime quarters and fish sauce in small bowls on a
platter, serve with the soup and allow your guests to help themselves.

INGREDIENTS

1 tablespoon olive oil
1 onion, sliced
$1/2$ teaspoon ground cumin
$1/2$ teaspoon paprika
1 teaspoon grated fresh ginger
1 clove garlic, crushed
2 celery sticks, sliced
2 small carrots, sliced
2 zucchini, sliced
1.125 litres chicken stock
2 chicken breast fillets, sliced
pinch saffron threads, optional
$1/2$ cup (95 g/3 oz) instant couscous
2 tablespoons chopped fresh parsley

1   Heat the oil in a large heavy-based pan. Add the onion and cook over medium heat for
    10 minutes, or until very soft, stirring occasionally. Add the cumin, paprika, ginger and
    garlic and cook, stirring, for 1 minute further.

2   Add the celery, carrot and zucchini and stir to coat with the spices. Stir in the stock. Bring
    to the boil, then reduce the heat and simmer, partially covered, for about 15 minutes, or
    until the vegetables are tender.

3   Add the chicken and saffron to the pan and cook for about 5 minutes, or until the chicken
    is just tender; do not overcook. Stir in the couscous and chopped parsley and serve.

INGREDIENTS

5 x 2 cm (2 x $^3/_4$ in) piece fresh galangal, peeled and cut into thin slices
500 ml (2 cups) coconut milk
250 ml (1 cup) chicken stock
4 fresh kaffir lime (makrut) leaves, torn
1 tablespoon finely chopped fresh coriander (cilantro) roots
500 g (1 lb 2 oz) chicken breast fillets, cut into thin strips
1–2 teaspoons finely chopped fresh red chillies
2 tablespoons fish sauce
1$^1/_2$ tablespoons lime juice
3 teaspoons palm sugar or soft brown sugar
4 tablespoons fresh coriander (cilantro) leaves

1   Place the galangal in a saucepan with the coconut milk, stock, lime leaves and coriander roots. Bring to the boil, reduce the heat to low and simmer for 10 minutes, stirring occasionally.

2   Add the chicken and chilli to the pan and simmer for 8 minutes.

3   Stir in the fish sauce, lime juice and palm sugar and cook for 1 minute. Stir in the coriander leaves. Serve immediately garnished with extra coriander, if desired.

INGREDIENTS

1.5 kg (2¹/₂ lb) chicken
2 carrots, roughly chopped
2 sticks celery, roughly chopped
1 onion, quartered
4 parsley sprigs
2 bay leaves
4 black peppercorns
50 g (1³/₄ oz) butter
2 tablespoons plain (all-purpose) flour
2 potatoes, chopped
250 g (8 oz) butternut pumpkin (squash), chopped into bite-sized pieces
2 carrots, extra, cut into matchsticks
1 leek, cut into matchsticks
3 sticks celery, extra, cut into matchsticks
100 g (3¹/₂ oz) green beans, cut into short lengths or baby green beans, halved
200 g (6¹/₂ oz) broccoli, cut into small florets
100 g (3¹/₂ oz) sugar snap peas, trimmed
50 g (1³/₄ oz) English spinach leaves, shredded
¹/₂ cup (125 ml/4 fl oz) cream
¹/₄ cup (15 g/¹/₂ oz) chopped parsley

1 To make the chicken stock, place the chicken in a large pan with the carrot, celery, onion, parsley, bay leaves, 2 teaspoons of salt and the peppercorns. Add 3 litres of water. Bring to the boil, reduce the heat and simmer for 1 hour, skimming the surface as required. Allow to cool for at least 30 minutes. Strain and reserve the liquid.

2 Remove the chicken and allow to cool enough to handle. Discard the skin, then cut or pull the flesh from the bones and shred into small pieces. Set the chicken meat aside.

3 Heat the butter in a large pan over medium heat and, when foaming, add the flour. Cook, stirring, for 1 minute. Remove from the heat and gradually stir in the stock. Return to the heat and bring to the boil, stirring continuously. Add the potato, pumpkin and extra carrot and simmer for 7 minutes. Add the leek, extra celery and beans and simmer for a further 5 minutes. Finally, add the broccoli and sugar snap peas and cook for a further 3 minutes.

4 Just before serving, add the chicken meat, spinach, cream and chopped parsley. Reheat gently but do not allow the soup to boil. Keep stirring until the spinach has wilted. Season to taste with plenty of salt and freshly ground black pepper. Serve immediately.

INGREDIENTS

10 g ($^1/_4$ oz) dried porcini mushrooms
25 g (1 oz) butter
1 leek (white part only), thinly sliced
250 g (9 oz) pancetta or bacon, chopped
200 g (7 oz) Swiss brown mushrooms, roughly chopped
300 g (10$^1/_2$ oz) large field mushrooms, roughly chopped
2 tablespoons plain (all-purpose) flour
125 ml ($^1/_2$ cup) Madeira
1.25 litres (5 cups) chicken stock
1 tablespoon olive oil
2 chicken breast fillets (about 200 g/7 oz each)
80 g ($^1/_3$ cup) light sour cream
2 teaspoons chopped marjoram, plus whole leaves, to garnish

1   Soak the porcini in 250 ml (1 cup) boiling water for 20 minutes.

2   Melt the butter in a large saucepan over medium heat and cook the leek and pancetta for 5 minutes, or until the leek is softened. Add all the mushrooms and the porcini soaking liquid and cook for 10 minutes.

3   Stir in the flour and cook for 1 minute. Add the Madeira and cook, stirring, for 10 minutes. Stir in the stock, bring to the boil, then reduce the heat and simmer for 45 minutes. Cool slightly.

4   Heat the oil in a frying pan and cook the chicken fillets for 4–5 minutes each side, or until cooked through. Remove from the pan and thinly slice.

5   Blend the soup until smooth. Return to the cleaned saucepan, add the sour cream and chopped marjoram and stir over medium heat for about 1–2 minutes to warm through. Season. Top with the chicken and garnish with marjoram.

180 g (6 oz) dried chickpeas
300 g (10 oz) smoked bacon ribs
2 tablespoons olive oil
1 onion, finely chopped
1 clove garlic, crushed
2 tomatoes, peeled, seeded and finely chopped
1 potato, cubed
1 carrot, sliced
200 g (6$^1/_2$ oz) pumpkin, chopped
150 g (5 oz) chorizo or pepperoni sausage, sliced
$^1/_4$ teaspoon dried oregano
6 cups (1.5 litres) chicken stock

1 Soak the chickpeas in cold water overnight. Drain.

2 Blanch bacon ribs in boiling water for 30 seconds, then plunge into iced water. Drain and slice into pieces.

3 Heat the oil in a large, heavy-based pan and cook the onion over medium heat for 3–4 minutes, stirring continuously. Add the garlic and tomato and cook for a further 5 minutes.

4 Add the chickpeas, ribs, potato, carrot, pumpkin, chorizo, dried oregano and stock. Bring to the boil, then reduce the heat and simmer, covered, for 30 minutes, or until the chickpeas are tender. Season to taste.

CHICKPEA, CHORIZO AND PORK RIB SOUP

CREAMY CHICKEN AND CORN SOUP

INGREDIENTS

20 g ($^3/_4$ oz) butter
1 tablespoon olive oil
500 g (1 lb 2 oz) chicken thigh fillets, trimmed and thinly sliced
2 garlic cloves, chopped
1 leek, chopped
1 large celery stalk, chopped
1 bay leaf
$^1/_2$ teaspoon thyme
1 litre (4 cups) chicken stock
60 ml ($^1/_4$ cup) sherry
550 g (1 lb 4 oz) corn kernels (fresh, canned or frozen)
1 large floury potato (russet), cut into 1 cm ($^1/_2$ in) cubes
185 ml ($^3/_4$ cup) cream, plus extra, to drizzle
chives, to garnish

1   Melt the butter and oil in a large saucepan over high heat. Cook the chicken in batches for 3 minutes, or until lightly golden and just cooked through. Place in a bowl, cover and refrigerate until needed.

2   Reduce the heat to medium and stir in the garlic, leek, celery, bay leaf and thyme. Cook for 2 minutes, or until the leek softens — do not allow the garlic to burn. Add the stock, sherry and 500 ml (2 cups) water and stir, scraping up any sediment stuck to the bottom of the pan. Add the corn and potato and bring to the boil. Reduce the heat and simmer for 1 hour, skimming any scum off the surface. Cool slightly.

3   Remove the bay leaf and purée the soup. Return to the cleaned pan, add the cream and chicken and stir over medium–low heat for 2–3 minutes, or until heated through — do not boil. Season. Drizzle with extra cream and garnish with chives. If desired, serve with crusty bread.

INGREDIENTS

3 dried shiitake mushrooms
1 Chinese roast duck (1.5 kg/3 lb 5 oz)
500 ml (2 cups) chicken stock
2 tablespoons light soy sauce
1 tablespoon Chinese rice wine
2 teaspoons sugar
400 g (14 oz) fresh flat rice noodles
2 tablespoons oil
3 spring onions (scallions), thinly sliced
1 teaspoon finely chopped ginger
400 g (14 oz) bok choy (pak choi), trimmed and leaves separated
$^1/_4$ teaspoon sesame oil

1 Place the shiitake mushrooms in a heatproof bowl, cover with 250 ml (1 cup) boiling water and soak for 20 minutes. Drain, reserving the liquid and squeezing the excess liquid from the mushrooms. Discard the woody stems and thinly slice the caps.

2 Remove the skin and flesh from the roast duck. Discard the fat and carcass. Finely slice the duck meat and the skin.

3 Place the chicken stock, soy sauce, rice wine, sugar and the reserved mushroom liquid in a saucepan over medium heat. Bring to a simmer and cook for 5 minutes. Meanwhile, place the rice noodles in a heatproof bowl, cover with boiling water and soak briefly. Gently separate the noodles with your hands and drain well. Divide evenly among large soup bowls.

4 Heat the oil in a wok over high heat. Add the spring onion, ginger and shiitake mushrooms and cook for several seconds. Transfer to the broth with the bok choy and duck meat and simmer for 1 minute, or until the duck has warmed through and the bok choy has wilted. Ladle the soup over the noodles and drizzle sesame oil on each serving. Serve immediately.

FIVE-SPICE DUCK AND SOMEN NOODLE SOUP

4 duck breasts, skin on
1 teaspoon five-spice powder
1 teaspoon peanut oil
200 g (7 oz) dried somen noodles

Star anise broth
1 litre (4 cups) chicken stock
3 whole star anise
5 spring onions (scallions), chopped
15 g (1/4 cup) chopped fresh coriander (cilantro) leaves

1 Preheat the oven to moderately hot 200°C (400°F/Gas 6). Trim the duck breast of excess fat, then lightly sprinkle both sides with the five-spice powder.

2 Heat the oil in a large frying pan. Add the duck skin-side down and cook over medium heat for 2–3 minutes, or until brown and crisp. Turn and cook the other side for 3 minutes. Transfer to a baking tray and cook, skin-side up, for another 8–10 minutes, or until cooked to your liking.

3 Meanwhile, place the chicken stock and star anise in a small saucepan. Bring to the boil, then reduce the heat and simmer for 5 minutes. Add the spring onion and coriander and simmer for 5 minutes.

4 Cook the noodles in a saucepan of boiling water for 2 minutes, or until soft. Drain and divide among four bowls. Ladle the broth on the noodles and top each bowl with one sliced duck breast.

INGREDIENTS

500 g (1 lb 2 oz) Italian pork sausages

200 g (7 oz) piece speck (see note)

1 tablespoon olive oil

1 large onion, chopped

3 garlic cloves, crushed

1 celery stalk, cut in half and sliced

1 large carrot, cut into 1 cm ($^1/_2$ in) cubes

bouquet garni (1 parsley sprig, 1 oregano sprig, 2 bay leaves)

1 small red chilli, halved lengthways

400 g (14 oz) can chopped tomatoes

1.75 litres (7 cups) chicken stock

300 g (10$^1/_2$ oz) Brussels sprouts, cut in half from top to base

300 g (10$^1/_2$ oz) green beans, cut into 3 cm (1$^1/_4$ inch) lengths

300 g (10$^1/_2$ oz) shelled broad beans, fresh or frozen

2 tablespoons chopped flat-leaf (Italian) parsley

1 Grill (broil) the sausages under a hot grill (broiler) for 8–10 minutes, turning occasionally, or until brown. Remove and cut into 3 cm (1$^1/_4$ in) lengths. Trim and reserve the fat from the speck, then dice the speck.

2 Heat the oil in a large saucepan over medium heat. Add the speck and reserved speck fat and cook for 2–3 minutes, or until golden. Add the onion, garlic, celery and carrot, reduce the heat to low and cook for 6–8 minutes, or until softened. Discard the remains of the speck fat.

3 Stir in the sausages, bouquet garni, chilli and chopped tomato and cook for 5 minutes. Add the stock, bring to the boil, then reduce the heat and simmer for 1 hour. Add the Brussels sprouts, green beans and broad beans and simmer for 30 minutes. Discard the bouquet garni, then stir in the parsley. Season to taste. Divide among four bowls and serve.

NOTE Speck is cured smoked ham or pork belly. It has a strong taste and is usually cut into small pieces and used as a flavour base.

1 litre (4 cups) beef stock
2 stems lemon grass, white part only, halved
3 garlic cloves, halved
2.5 x 2.5 cm (1 x 1 in) piece ginger, sliced
90 g (1 bunch) coriander (cilantro), leaves and stalks separated, leaves chopped
4 spring onions (scallions), thinly sliced on the diagonal
2 strips of 1.5 x 4 cm ($^5/_8$ x $1^1/_2$ in) lime zest
2 star anise
3 small red chillies, seeded and finely chopped
500 g (1 lb 2 oz) fillet steak, trimmed
2 tablespoons fish sauce
1 tablespoon grated palm sugar or soft brown sugar
2 tablespoons lime juice
coriander (cilantro) leaves, extra, to garnish

1 Place the stock, lemon grass, garlic, ginger, coriander stalks, 2 spring onions, the lime zest, star anise, 1 teaspoon of the chopped chilli and 1 litre (4 cups) water in a saucepan. Bring to the boil and simmer, covered, for 25 minutes. Strain and return the liquid to the pan.

2 Heat a chargrill pan (griddle) until very hot. Brush lightly with olive oil and sear the steak on both sides until browned on the outside, but very rare in the centre.

3 Reheat the soup, adding the fish sauce and palm sugar. Season with salt and black pepper. Add the lime juice to taste (you may want more than 2 tablespoons) — you should achieve a hot and sour flavour.

4 Add the remaining spring onion and the chopped coriander leaves to the soup. Slice the beef across the grain into thin strips. Curl the strips into a decorative pattern, then place in the centre of four deep serving bowls. Pour the soup over the beef and garnish with the remaining chilli and a few extra coriander leaves.

2 stems lemon grass, white part finely chopped, stem ends reserved and halved

6 cloves garlic, chopped

3 red Asian shallots, chopped

8 black peppercorns

1 teaspoon ready-made red curry paste

1 cup (250 ml/8 fl oz) coconut cream

400 ml (13^1/$_2$ fl oz) coconut milk

400 ml (13^1/$_2$ fl oz) chicken stock

2^1/$_2$ tablespoons thinly sliced fresh galangal

7 kaffir lime (makrut) leaves, shredded

400 g (14 oz) chicken breast fillets or thigh fillets, thinly sliced

2 tablespoons lime juice

2 tablespoons fish sauce

1 teaspoon grated palm sugar or soft brown sugar

3 tablespoons fresh coriander (cilantro) leaves

1 small fresh red chilli, thinly sliced

1   Process the chopped lemon grass, garlic, shallots, peppercorns and curry paste in a food processor to form a paste.

2   Heat a wok over low heat, add the coconut cream, increase the heat to high and bring to the boil. Add the paste and cook, stirring, for 5 minutes. Add the coconut milk and stock, return to the boil and add the sliced galangal, the kaffir lime leaves and reserved lemon grass stems. Reduce the heat and simmer for 5 minutes.

3   Add the chicken and simmer for 8 minutes, or until cooked. Stir in the lime juice, fish sauce, palm sugar, coriander leaves and chilli. Serve immediately.

THAI-STYLE CHICKEN AND COCONUT SOUP

JUNGLE SOUP

2 teaspoons oil
1 medium onion, finely sliced
225 g (8 oz) butternut pumpkin (squash), peeled and diced
225 g (8 oz) fresh pineapple or mango, chopped
1 garlic clove, crushed
1 dried red chilli, finely chopped
2 teaspoons grated ginger
1 litre (4 cups) chicken stock
2 tablespoons lime juice
350 g (12 oz) chicken breast, skinned, cut diagonally into thin strips

1   Heat the oil in a large heavy-based pan and cook the onion for 5 minutes, or until golden. Add the pumpkin and cook for 5 minutes, or until just brown. Add the pineapple, garlic, chilli and ginger and toss together.

2   Add the stock and lime juice, bring to the boil and then reduce the heat to simmer for 20 minutes, or until the pumpkin is nearly tender.

3   Add the chicken and simmer for 5 minutes, or until the chicken is cooked. Serve immediately.

INGREDIENTS

2 tablespoons oil
500 g (1 lb) lean lamb meat, cut into bite-sized cubes
2 onions, finely chopped
2 carrots, chopped
4 celery stalks, chopped
425 g (14 oz) can crushed tomatoes
2 litres beef stock
300 g (10 oz) spiral pasta
chopped fresh parsley, for serving

1 Heat the oil in a large pan and cook the lamb in batches until golden brown. Remove each batch as it is cooked and drain on paper towels. Add the onion to the pan and cook for 2 minutes or until softened. Return all the meat to the pan.

2 Add the carrot, celery, tomato and beef stock. Stir to combine and bring to the boil. Reduce the heat to low and simmer, covered, for 15 minutes.

3 Add the spiral pasta to the soup. Stir briefly to prevent the pasta sticking to the pan. Simmer, uncovered, for another 15 minutes or until the lamb and pasta are tender. Sprinkle with chopped parsley before serving.

LEMON CHICKEN SOUP

2 chicken breast fillets
1 lemon
1 litre chicken stock (see hint)
2 fresh lemon thyme sprigs, plus extra, to serve (see note)

1 Trim any excess fat from the chicken. Using a vegetable peeler, cut 2 strips of rind from the lemon and remove the pith. Place the stock, rind and lemon thyme in a shallow pan and slowly bring almost to the boil. Reduce to simmering point, add the chicken and cook, covered, for 7 minutes, or until the meat is tender.

2 Remove the chicken from the pan, transfer to a plate and cover with foil.

3 Strain the stock into a clean pan through a sieve lined with 2 layers of damp muslin. Finely shred the chicken and return to the soup. Reheat gently and season to taste with salt and freshly ground black pepper. Serve immediately, garnished with the extra sprigs of lemon thyme.

NOTE You can use ordinary thyme if lemon thyme is not available.

HINT If you don't have time to make your own stock, poultry shops or butchers sometimes sell their own. These may have more flavour and contain less salt than stock cubes.

500 g (1lb) chicken thigh fillets, excess fat removed
2 tablespoons plain (all-purpose) flour
1 tablespoon curry powder
1 teaspoon ground turmeric
30 g (1 oz butter)
1 onion, finely chopped
1 apple, peeled cored and finely chopped
4 cups (1 litre) chicken stock
6 whole cloves
⅓ cup (64 g/2¼ oz) basmati rice
1 tablespoon lemon juice
¼ cup (60 ml/2 fl oz) cream

1 Coat the chicken in the combined plain flour, curry powder and turmeric. Heat half the butter in a large pan and cook the chicken over medium heat for 3–4 minutes, or until lightly browned; turn frequently. Remove from the pan and drain on paper towels.

2 Add the remaining butter to the pan, then add the onion, apple and remaining flour mixture and cook for 3 minutes, or until soft. Return the chicken to the pan along with the stock and cloves. Bring to the boil, reduce the heat and simmer, covered, for 1 hour. Add the rice during the last 15 minutes and cook until it is tender.

3 Remove the chicken; allow to cool slightly and chop finely. Remove the cloves and skim any oil from the surface. Return the chicken to the pan. Reheat gently, stir in the lemon juice and cream, but do not allow the soup to boil. Season to taste with salt and freshly ground black pepper.

MULLIGATAWNY SOUP

INGREDIENTS

2 kg (4 lb 8 oz) oxtails, trimmed
2 tablespoons vegetable oil
2 onions, finely chopped
1 leek, finely chopped
2 carrots, diced
1 celery stalk, diced
2 garlic cloves, crushed
2 bay leaves
2 tablespoons tomato paste (purée)
1 thyme sprig
2 flat-leaf (Italian) parsley sprigs
3.5 litres (14 cups) chicken stock
375 ml (1 1/2 cups) stout
2 tomatoes, seeded and diced
100 g (3 1/2 oz) cauliflower florets
100 g (3 1/2 oz) green beans
100 g (3 1/2 oz) broccoli florets
100 g (3 1/2 oz) asparagus, cut into 3 cm (1 1/4 inch) lengths

1   Preheat the oven to 200°C (400°F/Gas 6). Place the oxtails in a baking dish and bake for
    1 hour, turning occasionally, or until dark golden. Leave to cool.

2   Heat the oil in a large saucepan over medium heat and cook the onion, leek, carrot and
    celery for 3–4 minutes, or until soft. Stir in the garlic, bay leaves and tomato paste, then
    add the oxtails, thyme and parsley.

3   Add the stock and bring to the boil over high heat. Reduce the heat and simmer for
    3 hours, or until the oxtails are tender and the meat falls off the bone. Skim off any scum
    that rises to the surface. Remove the oxtails and cool slightly.

4   Take the meat off the bones and discard any fat or sinew. Roughly chop and add to the
    soup with the stout, tomato and 500 ml (2 cups) water. Add the vegetables and simmer
    for 5 minutes, or until the vegetables are tender. Season.

1 tablespoon oil

2 onions, diced

2 carrots, diced

2 sticks celery, diced

1 parsnip, diced

1^1/$_2$ cups (330 g/10^1/$_2$ oz) green split peas

1 teaspoon black peppercorns

2 teaspoons dried thyme leaves

1 ham hock (850 g/1 lb 12 oz), cut into smaller pieces (ask your butcher to do this)

1   Heat the oil in a large pan and add the onion, carrot, celery and parsnip. Cook over low heat for 10 minutes, or until the vegetables have softened and the onion is translucent.

2   Add the split peas, peppercorns, thyme, the pieces of ham hock and 8 cups (2 litres) of water. Slowly bring to the boil, reduce the heat to low and simmer, covered, for 2^1/$_2$ hours, or until most of the meat has fallen off the bones and the vegetables and split peas are very soft. Stir occasionally.

3   Remove the bones from the pan, pulling off any of the meat that hasn't fallen away. Chop any large pieces and return to the pan. Season well with salt and pepper, if necessary.

INGREDIENTS

200 g (7 oz) Chinese barbecued pork (char sui) fillet in one piece
2 small fresh corn cobs (550 g/1 lb 4 oz)
200 g (7 oz) dried ramen noodles
2 teaspoons peanut oil
1 teaspoon grated ginger
1.5 litres (6 cups) chicken stock
2 tablespoons mirin
2 spring onions (scallions), sliced on the diagonal
20 g ($^3/_4$ oz) unsalted butter
1 spring onion, extra, sliced on the diagonal
Cut the pork into thin slices and remove the corn kernels from the cob using a sharp knife.

1   Bring a large saucepan of water to the boil, add the ramen noodles and cook for 4 minutes, or until tender. Drain, then rinse in cold water.

2   Heat the oil in a large saucepan over high heat. Stir-fry the grated ginger for 1 minute. Add the chicken stock and mirin and bring to the boil. Reduce the heat and simmer for 8 minutes.

3   Add the pork slices to the liquid and cook for 5 minutes, then add the corn kernels and spring onion and cook for a further 4–5 minutes, or until the kernels are tender.

4   Separate the noodles by running them under hot water, then divide among four deep bowls. Ladle on the soup, then place 1 teaspoon butter on each serving. Garnish with the extra spring onion and serve at once.

NOTE   This soup is traditionally served with the butter on top. However, for a healthier option, it is also quite delicious without the butter.

INGREDIENTS

300 g (1¹/₂ cups) long-grain rice, thoroughly rinsed
¹/₂ star anise
2 spring onions (scallions), white part only
4 x 4 cm (1¹/₂ x 1¹/₂ inch) piece ginger, cut into slices
3.5 litres (14 cups) chicken stock
1 tablespoon peanut oil
2 garlic cloves, crushed
1 teaspoon grated ginger, extra
400 g (14 oz) minced (ground) pork
ground white pepper
60 ml (¹/₄ cup) light soy sauce
sesame oil, to drizzle
6 fried dough sticks (see note)

1   Put the rice in a large saucepan with the star anise, spring onions, sliced ginger and chicken stock. Bring to the boil, then reduce the heat to low and simmer for 1¹/₂ hours, stirring occasionally.

2   Heat the oil in a frying pan over high heat. Cook the garlic and grated ginger for 30 seconds. Add the mince and cook for 5 minutes, or until browned, breaking up any lumps with the back of a spoon.

3   Remove the star anise, spring onions and ginger from the soup and discard them. Add the mince mixture and simmer for 10 minutes. Season with white pepper and stir in the soy sauce. Serve with a drizzle of sesame oil and the dough sticks.

NOTE   Fried dough sticks are available at Chinese bakeries and speciality shops and are best eaten soon after purchasing. If not, reheat in a 200°C (400°F/Gas 6) oven for 5 minutes, then serve.

2 tablespoons olive oil

8 lamb shanks

2 onions, sliced

4 cloves garlic, finely chopped

3 bay leaves, torn in half

1–2 teaspoons hot paprika

2 teaspoons sweet paprika

1 tablespoon plain (all-purpose) flour

3 tablespoons tomato paste (purée)

6 cups (1.5 litres) vegetable stock

4 potatoes, chopped

4 carrots, sliced

3 sticks celery, thickly sliced

3 tomatoes, seeded and chopped

1 To make lamb stock, heat 1 tablespoon of the oil in a large, heavy-based pan over medium heat. Brown the shanks well in two batches and drain on paper towels.

2 Add remaining tablespoon of oil to pan and cook onion, garlic and bay leaves over low heat for 10 minutes, stirring regularly. Add paprikas and flour and cook, stirring, for 2 minutes. Gradually add combined tomato paste and stock. Bring to the boil, stirring, and return shanks to the pan. Reduce heat to low and simmer, covered, for 1$\frac{1}{2}$ hours, stirring occasionally.

3 Remove bay leaves and discard. Remove shanks, allow to cool slightly and then cut the meat from the bone. Discard bones. Cut meat into pieces and refrigerate. Refrigerate stock for about 1 hour, or until fat forms on surface and can be spooned off.

4 Return the meat to the soup along with the potato, carrot and celery and bring to the boil. Reduce the heat and simmer for 15 minutes. Season and add the chopped tomato to serve.

INGREDIENTS

1 kg (2 lb) lamb shanks, cut in half through the bone (ask your butcher to do this)
3 onions, chopped
3 turnips, chopped
2 carrots, chopped
1 tablespoon black peppercorns
$^1/_2$ cup (110 g/3$^1/_2$ oz) pearl barley
1 carrot, diced, extra
2 onions, finely chopped, extra
1 leek, chopped
1 stick celery, diced
2 turnips, diced, extra
chopped flat-leaf parsley

1   To make the stock, put the lamb shanks, onion, turnip, carrot, pepper-corns and 8 cups
    (2 litres) of water in a large pan. Bring to the boil, reduce the heat and simmer, covered,
    for 3 hours. Skim the surface as required.

2   Remove the shanks and any meat that has fallen off the bones and cool slightly. Remove
    the meat from the bones and finely chop, then cover and refrigerate. Strain the stock,
    discarding the vegetables. Cool the stock and refrigerate overnight, or until the fat has set
    on top and can be spooned off. Cover the barley with water and soak for 1 hour.

3   Put the stock in a large pan and gently reheat. Add the drained barley, extra carrot, onion,
    leek, celery and turnip. Bring to the boil, reduce the heat and simmer for 30 minutes, or
    until the barley and vegetables are just cooked. Return the meat to the pan and simmer
    for 5 minutes. Season well and serve with the parsley.

INGREDIENTS

150 g (5¹/₂ oz) spaghetti, broken into 8 cm (3 in) lengths
1.5 litres (6 cups) beef stock
3 teaspoons tomato paste (purée)
400 g (14 oz) can chopped tomatoes
3 tablespoons basil leaves, torn
shaved Parmesan cheese, to garnish

Meatballs
1 tablespoon oil
1 onion, finely chopped
2 garlic cloves, crushed
500 g (1 lb 2 oz) lean minced (ground) beef
3 tablespoons finely chopped flat-leaf (Italian) parsley
3 tablespoons fresh breadcrumbs
2 tablespoons finely grated Parmesan cheese
1 egg, lightly beaten

1 Cook the spaghetti in a large saucepan of boiling water according to packet instructions until al dente. Drain. Put the stock and 500 ml (2 cups) water in a large saucepan and slowly bring to a simmer.

2 Meanwhile, to make the meatballs, heat the oil in a small frying pan over medium heat and cook the onion for 2–3 minutes, or until soft. Add the garlic and cook for 30 seconds. Allow to cool.

3 Combine the mince, parsley, breadcrumbs, Parmesan, egg, the onion mixture, and salt and pepper. Roll a heaped teaspoon of mixture into a ball, making 40 balls in total.

4 Stir the tomato paste and tomato into the beef stock and simmer for 2–3 minutes. Drop in the meatballs, return to a simmer and cook for 10 minutes, or until cooked through. Stir in the spaghetti and basil to warm through. Season, garnish with shaved Parmesan and serve.

INGREDIENTS

350 g (11 oz) chicken thighs or wings, skin removed
2 carrots, finely chopped
2 celery sticks, finely chopped
2 small leeks, finely chopped
3 egg whites
1.5 litres chicken stock
Tabasco sauce

Coriander Pasta
$^1/_2$ cup (60 g/2 oz) plain (all-purpose) flour
1 egg
$^1/_2$ teaspoon sesame oil
small bunch coriander (cilantro) leaves

1 Put the chicken, carrot, celery and leek in a large heavy-based pan. Push the chicken to one side and add the egg whites to the vegetables. Using a wire whisk, beat for 1 minute, or until frothy (take care not to use a pan that can be scratched by the whisk).

2 Warm the stock in another pan, then add gradually to the first pan, whisking constantly to froth the egg whites. Continue whisking while slowly bringing to the boil. Make a hole in the top of the froth with a spoon and leave to simmer, uncovered, for 30 minutes without stirring.

3 Line a large strainer with a damp tea towel or double thickness of muslin and strain the broth into a clean bowl. Discard the chicken pieces and vegetables. Season to taste with salt, ground black pepper and Tabasco sauce. Set aside.

4 To make the coriander pasta, sift the flour into a bowl and make a well in the centre. Whisk the egg and oil together and pour into the well. Mix together to make a soft pasta dough and knead on a lightly floured surface for 2 minutes, or until smooth.

5 Divide the pasta dough into four even portions. Roll one portion out very thinly and cover with a layer of evenly spaced coriander leaves. Roll out another portion of pasta and lay this on top of the leaves, then gently roll the layers together. Repeat with the remaining pasta and coriander.

6 Cut out squares of pasta around the coriander leaves. The pasta may then be left to sit and dry out if it is not needed immediately. Just before serving, heat the chicken broth gently in a saucepan. As the broth simmers, add the pasta and cook for 1 minute. Serve immediately.

SPICY CHICKEN BROTH WITH CORIANDER PASTA

INGREDIENTS

2 large onions, roughly chopped

3 red chillies, seeded, chopped (or 2 teaspoons dried chilli)

3–4 garlic cloves

2 cm ($^3/_4$ inch) piece ginger, chopped

1 teaspoon ground black pepper

6 cm ($2^1/_2$ inch) piece lemon grass, white only, chopped

$^1/_2$ teaspoon ground cardamom

2 teaspoons ground cumin

$^1/_2$ teaspoon ground cinnamon

1 teaspoon ground turmeric

2 tablespoons peanut oil

1.5 kg (3 lb 5 oz) lamb neck chops

2–3 tablespoons vindaloo paste

580 ml ($2^1/_3$ cups) coconut cream

45 g ($^1/_4$ cup) soft brown sugar

2–3 tablespoons lime juice

4 kaffir lime (makrut) leaves

1   Put the onion, chilli, garlic, ginger, pepper, lemon grass and spices in a food processor. Process to a paste. Heat half the oil in a large pan and brown the chops in batches. Remove.

2   Add the remaining oil to the pan and cook the spice and vindaloo pastes for 2–3 minutes. Add the chops and 1.75 litres (7 cups) water, cover and bring to the boil. Reduce the heat; simmer, covered, for 1 hour. Remove the chops from the pan and stir in the coconut cream. Remove the meat from the bones, shred and return to the pan.

3   Add the sugar, lime juice and leaves. Simmer, uncovered, over low heat for 20–25 minutes, until slightly thickened. Garnish with coriander (cilantro).

5 cm (2 inch) piece of fresh galangal or 5 slices of dried galangal

6 kaffir lime (makrut) leaves

1 stem lemon grass, white part only, quartered

2 cups (500 ml/16 fl oz) coconut milk

2 cups (500 ml/16 fl oz) chicken stock

3 chicken breast fillets, cut into thin strips

1–2 teaspoons finely chopped red chillies

$^1/_4$ cup (60 ml/2 fl oz) lime juice

2 tablespoons fish sauce

1 teaspoon soft brown sugar

$^1/_4$ cup (15 g/$^1/_2$ oz) coriander (cilantro) leaves

1   Peel the galangal and cut into thin slices. Mix the galangal, kaffir lime leaves and lemon grass with the coconut milk and stock in a medium pan. Bring to the boil, reduce the heat to low and simmer for 10 minutes, stirring occasionally.

2   Add the chicken strips and chilli and simmer for 8 minutes. Mix in the lime juice, fish sauce and sugar. Serve with the coriander leaves and garnish with coriander sprigs, if you want.

TOM KHA GAI

INGREDIENTS

400 g (14 oz) rump steak, trimmed
¹/₂ onion
1¹/₂ tablespoons fish sauce
1 star anise
1 cinnamon stick
pinch ground white pepper
1.5 litres (6 cups) beef stock
300 g (10¹/₂ oz) fresh thin rice noodles
3 spring onions (scallions), thinly sliced
15 g (³/₄ cup) Vietnamese mint leaves
90 g (1 cup) bean sprouts
1 small white onion, cut in half and thinly sliced
1 small red chilli, thinly sliced on the diagonal
lemon wedges, to serve

1 Wrap the rump steak in plastic wrap and freeze for 40 minutes.

2 Meanwhile, put the onion, fish sauce, star anise, cinnamon stick, pepper, stock and 500 ml (2 cups) water in a large saucepan. Bring to the boil, then reduce the heat, cover and simmer for 20 minutes. Discard the onion, star anise and cinnamon stick.

3 Cover the noodles with boiling water and gently separate the strands. Drain and refresh under cold water.

4 Remove the meat from the freezer and thinly slice it across the grain.

5 Divide the noodles and spring onion among four deep bowls. Top with the beef, mint, bean sprouts, onion and chilli. Ladle the hot broth over the top and serve with the lemon wedges.

INGREDIENTS

2 dried Chinese mushrooms

15 raw prawns (shrimp)

100 g (3^1/$_2$ oz) minced (ground) pork

2 spring onions, chopped

1 teaspoon grated ginger

2 tablespoons canned water chestnuts, chopped

2 teaspoons chopped lemon grass, white part only

1 clove garlic, finely chopped

3 tablespoons soy sauce

225 g (7 oz) won ton wrappers

coriander (cilantro) leaves

6 cups (1.5 litres) beef stock

3 baby carrots, cut diagonally

3 spring onions, cut diagonally

1 Soak the mushrooms in hot water for 30 minutes. Peel and devein the prawns, then cut in half lengthways. Drain the mushrooms, remove the stems and chop the caps.

2 Mix the chopped mushroom with the pork, spring onion, ginger, water chestnut, lemon grass, garlic and 1 tablespoon of the soy sauce. Work with 1 won ton wrapper at a time, keeping the rest covered. Put 2–3 coriander leaves, half a prawn and a heaped teaspoon of the pork mixture in the centre of a wrapper. Brush the edges with water and lay another wrapper on top. Press to seal. Repeat with the remaining wrappers.

3 Bring the stock, remaining soy sauce, carrot and spring onion to the boil. Bring another large pan of water to the boil and cook the won tons in batches for 4–5 minutes; drain. Pour the hot soup over the won tons.

AVGOLEMONO (GREEK EGG AND LEMON SOUP)

INGREDIENTS

1.5 litres (6 cups) chicken stock
150 g (³/₄ cup) long-grain rice
2 eggs, separated
125 ml (¹/₂ cup) lemon juice

1   Bring the stock to the boil in a large heavy-based pan. Add the rice and allow to simmer for 8–10 minutes until tender.

2   Beat the egg whites in a large dry mixing bowl until soft peaks form. Add the yolks and beat until they are combined.

3   Gradually pour in the lemon juice and then about 1–2 cups of the rice and stock soup, beating continuously. Gradually fold this into the pan of rice soup and serve immediately.

INGREDIENTS

30 g (1 oz) butter
4 rashers bacon, cut into strips
1 onion, finely chopped
$^1/_2$ teaspoon sweet paprika
1 kg (2 lb) potatoes, chopped
3 cups (750 ml/24 fl oz) chicken stock
1 cup (125 g/4 oz) grated Cheddar
chopped chives, to serve

1   Melt the butter in a large pan, add the bacon and cook until crisp. Remove the bacon from the pan with a slotted spoon, leaving as much fat as possible. Add the onion to the same pan and cook for 5 minutes, or until very soft and golden. Add the paprika and cook for a further 30 seconds.

2   Return the bacon to the pan and add the potato and stock. Bring to the boil, then reduce the heat and simmer for 30 minutes, or until the potato is very soft. Stir or mash lightly to break up the potato. Add the Cheddar and stir well, until it is melted through. Season with salt and pepper to taste and serve topped with a sprinkling of chopped chives.

STILTON AND APPLE SOUP

40 g (1¹/₂ oz) butter
2 tablespoons plain (all-purpose) flour
750 ml (3 cups) chicken stock
4 red apples
500 ml (2 cups) milk
250 g (9 oz) Stilton cheese
2 tablespoons chopped chives

1   Melt the butter in a large heavy-based pan. Sprinkle with the flour and stir over low heat for 2 minutes, or until lightly golden. Gradually add the stock, stirring until smooth.

2   Peel, core and slice the apples and add to the pan. Cook, covered, over medium heat for 20 minutes, or until tender. Cool, then purée in a processor in batches until smooth.

3   Return the soup to the pan, add the milk and reheat, stirring. Simmer gently and add the crumbled Stilton and chives. Stir until the soup is smooth and serve immediately.

1 small fresh red chilli, seeded and chopped

1 stem lemon grass, white part only, sliced

1 teaspoon ground coriander

1 tablespoon chopped fresh ginger

2 cups (500 ml) vegetable stock

2 tablespoons oil

1 onion, finely chopped

800 g pumpkin flesh, cubed

1 1/2 cups (375 ml) coconut milk

3 tablespoons chopped fresh coriander (cilantro) leaves

2 teaspoons shaved palm sugar or soft brown sugar

extra coriander (cilantro) leaves, to garnish

1   Place the chilli, lemon grass, ground coriander, ginger and 2 tablespoons vegetable stock in a food processor, and process until smooth.

2   Heat the oil in a large saucepan, add the onion and cook over medium heat for 5 minutes. Add the spice paste and cook, stirring, for 1 minute.

3   Add the pumpkin and remaining vegetable stock. Bring to the boil, then reduce the heat and simmer, covered, for 15–20 minutes, or until the pumpkin is tender. Cool slightly then process in a food processor or blender until smooth. Return to the cleaned pan, stir in the coconut milk, coriander and palm sugar, and simmer until hot. Garnish with the extra coriander leaves.

SPICY PUMPKIN AND COCONUT SOUP

INGREDIENTS

8 dried shiitake mushrooms
600 g chicken breast fillets, cut into 1.5 cm ($^1/_2$ inch) thick strips
$^1/_4$ cup (60 g/2 oz) white miso paste
2 teaspoons dashi granules
1 tablespoon wakame flakes or other seaweed (see note)
300 g (10$^1/_2$ oz) baby bok choy, halved lengthways
400 g (14 oz) fresh udon noodles
150 g (5$^1/_3$ oz) silken firm tofu, cut into 1 cm cubes
3 spring onions, sliced diagonally

1   Soak the mushrooms in 1 cup (250 ml) boiling water for 20 minutes. Drain, reserving the
    liquid; discard the stalks and thinly slice the caps.

2   Pour 2 litres water into a saucepan and bring to the boil, then reduce the heat and simmer.
    Add the chicken and cook for 2–3 minutes, or until almost cooked through.

3   Add the mushrooms and cook for 1 minute, then add the miso paste, dashi granules,
    wakame and reserved mushroom liquid. Stir to dissolve the dashi and miso paste.
    Do not boil.

4   Add the bok choy halves and simmer for 1 minute, or until beginning to wilt, then add the
    noodles and simmer for a further 2 minutes. Gently stir in the tofu and ladle the hot soup
    into large serving bowls. Garnish with the sliced spring onion.

    Wakame is a curly-leafed, brown algae with a mild vegetable taste and a soft texture. It
    can be used in salads or can be boiled and served like a vegetable. Use a small amount
    as it swells by about ten times after being cooked.

30 g (1 oz) butter
3 large onions, halved and thinly sliced
2 tablespoons firmly packed soft brown sugar
1 cup (250 ml/8 fl oz) dry white wine
3 large parsnips, peeled, chopped
1.25 (42 fl oz) litres vegetable stock
$^1/_4$ cup (60 ml/2 fl oz) cream
fresh thyme leaves, to garnish

1 Melt the butter in a large saucepan. Add the onion and sugar, and cook over low heat for
10 minutes. Add the wine and parsnip, and simmer, covered, for 20 minutes, or until the onion
and parsnip are golden and tender.

2 Pour in the stock, bring to the boil, then reduce the heat and simmer, covered, for 10 minutes.
Cool slightly, then place in a blender or food processor and blend in batches until smooth.
Season. Drizzle with a little cream and sprinkle fresh thyme leaves over the top. Serve with
toasted crusty bread slices.

CARAMELISED ONION AND PARSNIP SOUP

INGREDIENTS

375 g (13¹/₄ oz) fresh ramen noodles
1 tablespoon oil
1 tablespoon finely chopped fresh ginger
2 cloves garlic, crushed
150 g (5¹/₃ oz) oyster mushrooms, halved
1 small zucchini (courgette), sliced into thin rounds
1 leek, white and light green part, halved lengthways and thinly sliced
100 g (3¹/₂ oz) snow peas (mangetout), halved diagonally
100 g (3¹/₂ oz) fried tofu puffs, cut into matchsticks
5¹/₄ cups (1.25 litres/42¹/₄ fl oz) vegetable stock
1¹/₂ tablespoons white miso paste
2 tablespoons light soy sauce
1 tablespoon mirin
1 cup (90 g/3 oz) bean sprouts
1 teaspoon sesame oil
4 spring onions, thinly sliced
100 g (3¹/₂ oz) enoki mushrooms

1   Bring a large saucepan of lightly salted water to the boil. Add the noodles and cook, stirring to prevent sticking, for 4 minutes, or until just tender. Drain and rinse under cold running water.

2   Heat the oil in a large saucepan over medium heat, add the ginger, crushed garlic, oyster mushrooms, zucchini, leek, snow peas and tofu puffs, and stir-fry for 2 minutes. Add the stock and 300 ml water and bring to the boil, then reduce the heat and simmer. Stir in the miso, soy sauce and mirin until heated through. Do not boil. Stir in the bean sprouts and sesame oil.

3   Place the noodles in the bottom of six serving bowls, then pour in the soup. Garnish with the spring onion and enoki mushrooms.

INGREDIENTS

2 tablespoons olive oil

1 onion, chopped

2 cloves garlic, crushed

500 g (17$^1/_2$ oz) beef chuck steak, cut into 2 cm (1 inch) cubes

1 litre (34 fl oz) beef stock

2 small beetroot (250 g/9 oz)

200 g (7 oz) canned crushed tomatoes

1 carrot, diced

2 potatoes (280 g/10 oz), diced

2$^1/_2$ cups (190 g/6$^3/_4$ oz) finely shredded cabbage

2 teaspoons lemon juice

2 teaspoons sugar

2 tablespoons chopped fresh flat-leaf parsley

2 tablespoons chopped fresh dill

$^1/_3$ cup (90 g) sour cream

1 Preheat the oven to moderately hot 200°C (400°F/Gas 6). Heat the oil in a large saucepan, and cook the onion and garlic over medium heat for 3–5 minutes. Add the beef, stock and 1 litre water, and bring to the boil. Reduce the heat and simmer, covered, for 1 hour 15 minutes, or until the meat is tender. Remove the meat.

2 Trim the beetroot just above the end of the leaf stalks. Wrap in foil and bake for 30–40 minutes, or until tender. Unwrap and leave to cool.

3 Return the stock to the boil and add the tomato, carrot and potato, and season with salt. Cook over medium heat for 10 minutes. Add the cabbage and cook for 5 minutes. Peel and dice the beetroot. Return the meat to the pan and add the beetroot, lemon juice, sugar and 1$^1/_2$ tablespoons each of parsley and dill. Cook for 2 minutes, or until heated through. Season to taste.

4 Remove from the heat and leave for 10 minutes. Serve with a dollop of sour cream and garnish with the remaining dill and parsley.

All our recipes are thoroughly tested in a specially developed test kitchen. Standard metric measuring cups and spoons are used in the development of our recipes. All cup and spoon measurements are level. We have used 60 g (2¼ oz/Grade 3) eggs in all recipes. Sizes of cans vary from manufacturer to manufacturer and between countries – use the can size closest to the one suggested in the recipe.

CONVERSION GUIDE

1 cup = 250 ml (9 fl oz)

1 teaspoon = 5 ml

1 Australian tablespoon = 20 ml (4 teaspoons)

1 UK/US tablespoon = 15 ml (3 teaspoons)

DRY MEASURES

30 g = 1 oz

250 g = 9 oz

500 g = 1 lb 2 oz

LIQUID MEASURES

30 ml = 1 fl oz

125 ml = 4 fl oz

250 ml = 9 fl oz

LINEAR MEASURES

6 mm = ¼ inch

1 cm = ½ inch

2.5 cm = 1 inch

CUP CONVERSIONS – DRY INGREDIENTS

1 cup almonds, slivered whole = 125 g (4½ oz)

1 cup cheese, lightly packed processed cheddar = 155 g (5½ oz)

1 cup wheat flour = 125 g (4½ oz)

1 cup wholemeal flour = 140 g (5 oz)

1 cup minced (ground) meat = 250 g (9 oz)

1 cup pasta shapes = 125 g (4½ oz)

1 cup raisins = 170 g (6 oz)

1 cup rice, short grain, raw = 200 g (7 oz)

1 cup sesame seeds = 160 g (6 oz)

1 cup split peas = 250 g (9 oz)

INTERNATIONAL GLOSSARY

capsicum	sweet bell pepper
chick pea	garbanzo bean
chilli	chile, chili pepper
cornflour	cornstarch
eggplant	aubergine
spring onion	scallion
zucchini	courgette
plain flour	all-purpose flour
prawns	shrimp
minced meat	ground meat

Where temperature ranges are indicated, the lower figure applies to gas ovens, the higher to electric ovens. This allows for the fact that the flame in gas ovens generates a drier heat, which effectively cooks food faster than the moister heat of an electric oven, even if the temperature setting is the same.

	°C	°F	GAS MARK
Very slow	120	250	½
Slow	150	300	2
Mod slow	160	325	3
Moderate	180	350	4
Mod hot	190(g)–210(e)	375–425	5
Hot	200(g)–240(e)	400–475	6
Very hot	230(g)–260(e)	450–525	8

Published in 2006 by Bay Books,
an imprint of Murdoch Books Pty Limited.

ISBN 1-74045-825-7
978-1-74045-825-2

Printed by Sing Cheong Printing Company Ltd.
Printed in China.